PRAISE FOR *BETTER BARGAINING*

"*Better Bargaining: Navigating the Minefield of Collective Bargaining in the Public Sector* is a must read for every board member and administrator, whether or not they are directly involved in negotiations. Over his storied career, Nick Pittner has seen it all as a labor relations attorney. He takes us beyond theory into the real-life, hands-on world of collective bargaining where he translates a lifetime of lessons on understanding the process and the substantive issues for both the practitioner and the layman. From preparation, to negotiations, to impasse, to strike and beyond, Pittner prepares you for what lies ahead in your journey through the ins and outs of this complex field."

> Rick Lewis, Executive Director/CEO,
> Ohio School Boards Association

"While my bargaining experience with Nick Pittner was on the union side of the table, I have always had tremendous respect for his professionalism, respect for all parties, and commitment to getting to a mutually beneficial deal. This book provides a how-to guide for all who serve in any bargaining capacity on the management side, and I [also] encourage my labor colleagues to read it as a way to gain new insights into the process from various perspectives. Having participated in Interest Based Bargaining for two contracts with Nick, I especially share his enthusiasm for the IBB process. This is a great read from one of the most knowledgeable bargaining pros I know."

Scott DiMauro, President,
Ohio Education Association

"Because of Mr. Pittner's knowledge and experience in bargaining, this book is a must read for both would-be and active practitioners in the area."

George M. Albu,
Former Federal Mediator

"Nick Pittner writes from at least four decades of bargaining experience. His long involvement in hundreds of contract negotiations is a testament to his success. Bargainers would do well to heed the real-life experience and expertise provided in the book; to do otherwise would be at their own peril.

"Nick is also an expert in school finance, as evidenced by serving as lead attorney in the high-profile DeRolph School Funding case in Ohio. In a political environment that was stacked against the plaintiffs, Nick Pittner led a legal team that swayed the Ohio Supreme Court to rule in favor of the school district plaintiffs.

"This is a must-read book for those who would sit at the bargaining table."

William L. Phillis, Executive Director,
Ohio Coalition for Equity & Adequacy of School Funding

BETTER BARGAINING

NAVIGATING THE MINEFIELD OF PUBLIC SECTOR COLLECTIVE BARGAINING

NICHOLAS A. PITTNER

proving
press

Book Design & Production:
Columbus Publishing Lab
www.ColumbusPublishingLab.com

Copyright © 2023 by Nicholas A. Pittner
LCCN: 2022923582

Paperback ISBN: 978-1-63337-702-8
E-Book ISBN: 978-1-63337-703-5

Printed in the United States of America
1 3 5 7 9 10 8 6 4 2

To Susy, who made it possible.

Acknowledgments

Many people contributed to this work, and it is impossible to thank all of them by name. But, some who stand out include:

Robert T. (Bob) Baker, my first bargaining mentor, who taught that the essential qualities of a good negotiator are "a leather backside and rubber kidneys."

George M. Albu, the best mediator I've ever seen, who contributed a great deal of insight to this work.

Chris Bruhn, whose thoughtful edits and insightful suggestions made this work far better than it would otherwise have been.

Cassandra Casto, whose research and thoughtful comments contributed a great deal.

Amy Wilson, without whose assistance this work would not have been possible.

Mike Moses, who brought a far deeper understanding of some of the labor-side issues.

All of the clients whose contracts I've helped bargain over the past years.

DISCLAIMER

This work is not intended, and should not be considered or relied on, as legal advice on any matter. Collective bargaining is a complex process, often governed by both state and federal law and regulations. You should consult legal counsel in your jurisdiction for guidance on bargaining and related issues.

Table of Contents

Introduction

Chances are you're reading this because you have become responsible for the results of collective bargaining, and you want to know how it works. You've come to the right place. Whether elected or appointed to a governing board or chosen as a member of the management or union's bargaining team, you are about to be thrust into an unfamiliar process that may significantly impact the welfare of the enterprise for which you are responsible. In over thirty-five years of bargaining in the public sector, I've seen the consequences of many bargaining mistakes; both on the side of labor and management. Bargaining mistakes can adversely affect all of the parties. But more importantly, in the public sector they also affect the public served by the institution, with potential interruptions of service or loss of educational opportunity during a school strike.

The purpose of this book is to help you avoid those mistakes. First, by familiarizing you with the process—how it works, what it means, and how to navigate the bargaining minefield to a successful conclusion. It will also offer suggestions about what to do when the wheels come off and the process fails to work as it should. It is not a how-to-beat-'em book for either side of the bargaining process. Rather, it is intended to familiarize you with the process and offer insights on how to bargain to a successful conclusion that not only reaches agreement but also achieves your bargaining goals in the process. We will cover the entire gamut, from planning to completion—and beyond. Whether you are new to the process or a seasoned veteran, experience has taught me that most bargaining exercises can benefit from a better understanding of the concepts discussed in this book.

Bargaining is important because, presently the public sector is the most highly unionized segment of the United States labor market.[1] Unions want, and in many states have a lawful right, to bargain the wages, hours, and working conditions for their members, and collective bargaining is the process by which that happens. More importantly, the fact is that the public sector exists to provide governmental services to a segment of the public, and those services may well have a direct impact on the welfare of the entire community. For example, a teachers' strike can completely shut down a school district, leaving students without educational opportunities, and in some cases, a large segment of the community workforce without a paycheck. Collective bargaining matters, and its effects are felt throughout the entire community. Likewise, the funds that pay for public services are generally raised from local tax dollars, and a large portion of the cost of those services is determined by the collective bargaining process. As you can see, the results of collective bargaining can have a profound impact not only on the labor and management sides, but also on the wider community served by the entity engaging in the bargaining.

What follows will give you a deeper understanding of both the process and strategies to bring that process to a successful conclusion. We will cover the spectrum, from planning to actual bargaining sessions with a discussion of outcomes—both good and bad—as well as strategies to repair the process if it goes off the rails. Beyond the process itself, you will gain insight into building strong labor-management relations that will sustain your enterprise through the new labor contract and vastly simplify negotiations for the next one.

Because most of my personal bargaining experience involved public school districts in Ohio, they will serve as a reference point throughout. However, the bargaining issues and process is similar regardless of where it's carried out, and public sector collective bargaining is not unique either to Ohio or to public school districts. Presently, the majority of states permit collective bargaining for public-sector employees, many including police and firefighter units.[2] Although public-sector unions have been under assault in many states recently, the process of bargaining has gone on for a very long time and likely will continue into the future for most public employee unions and public entities.

A word of caution about police and fire (safety forces) collective bargaining. Because of the significant impact these services have on public welfare, many states have developed separate sets of rules governing safety forces bargaining. These rules can involve mandatory procedures for the resolution of wage disputes and prohibitions on the right to strike if agreement is not reached. In some cases, the mandatory procedures can significantly impact the bargaining strategies for both sides of the negotiations. Much of the general process and strategy discussed below may still be useful to those preparing for safety forces bargaining, but if your particular interest lies in that arena, please consult with your labor counsel before planning strategies based on the information presented here.

At its essence, there are two parts to collective bargaining—the bargaining process being followed and the substantive issues being bargained. Similarly, this book is divided into two parts. Part I is devoted to a description of the processes normally utilized in public sector bargaining. Equally important, however, is the substance of what is being bargained. The substance is defined by words, and words matter. Every word in a bargaining proposal helps define a right, benefit, or obligation that may become part of the final contract. We will review examples of some of the more common types of proposals and describe the interests of both labor and management in those proposals, as well as some pitfalls to avoid whenever possible. Due to the vast array of potential issues that can come up in bargaining, the discussion is limited to the most common—and often problematic—of those issues. First, let's talk about the players and the process.

CHAPTER 1

Getting to Know the Players

The two sides of any collective bargaining exercise can broadly be designated "labor" for the union side and "management" for the employer side. In the public sector, however, there can be numerous types of entities engaging in bargaining on the management side. For example, cities, counties, townships, school districts, and other components of local or state government can all be required (or permitted) to engage in collective bargaining with their employee groups. Regardless of the specific type of governmental entity, we will refer to the management side, the public sector employer, as the "enterprise." A public sector enterprise (a city, for example) could bargain with numerous different employee unions, but for our purposes here, it will still be referred to as the "enterprise" for purposes of the bargaining issues we will be discussing.

The other side of the labor/management equation is the labor side, which we will refer to here as the "union." The union side, however, may include all of the employees or just those in the particular bargaining unit that is conducting the bargaining. So, more definition is necessary.

BARGAINING UNIT. The term "bargaining unit" refers to that group of employees who are subject to the collective bargaining agreement being bargained. For example, all of the school bus drivers employed by a school district could represent a bargaining unit. Or, the unit could include all of the non-teaching employees of a particular school district or all of the non-supervisory members of the police force. Bargaining units can be task-focused, such as a unit consisting of only the school district cooks, or very broad such as a "wall-to-wall" unit that includes all of the non-management employees of the public employer. What's important to keep in mind here is that all of the employees within the bargaining unit are covered by the bargaining agreement and that the local union represents all of the employees in the bargaining unit, *whether they have chosen to join the local union or not.*

LOCAL UNION. The local union, often described, for example, as "Local xxx," is the local organization representing the employees described in the bargaining unit. The union is described as "local" because the local union is generally affiliated with and supported by much larger state, and often national, affiliate unions. For example, school teachers in Ohio are often members of local unions affiliated with the Ohio Education Association, which, in turn, is affiliated with the National Education Association. Some school bus driver units are affiliated with Teamsters International while other units may be affiliated with other state or national unions.

MANAGEMENT. When we refer to management here we are talking about those employees with management responsibility. Those responsibilities generally include the right to hire, fire, evaluate, and assign workers to specific job duties. Traditionally, management employees are excluded from bargaining units, though some may be authorized by law to form their own bargaining unit for limited negotiation purposes. Managers include, for example, school principals and the superintendent, as well as similarly titled supervisors in other governmental activities. They are not members of the bargaining unit, but as representatives of the governmental enterprise, they are bound to follow the collective bargaining agreement to the same extent as the enterprise.

GOVERNING BODY. The public sector enterprise's ultimate governance responsibility is assigned to variously named entities that exist because of legislation that causes them to exist. For example, boards of education govern school districts in many states. In Ohio, township trustees govern townships, boards of commissioners govern county government, and city councils, in many cities, govern city government. In other states, the terminology may well differ, but the common factor is that the governing body is ultimately responsible for the operations of the enterprise. Here, we will use "governing body" to describe the individual or group of individuals (board, commission, etc.) with the ultimate authority to agree to a collective bargaining agreement.

COLLECTIVE BARGAINING AGREEMENT. This is the term we will use to describe the contract that is the end result of the bargaining process. It is a contract, binding on the local union and the employee members of the bargaining unit on one side, and on the public entity that employs and manages those employees on the other. Collective bargaining agreements generally have fixed terms, often for not more than three years. The process by which the agreement is either initially agreed to or renewed is the focus of the bargaining discussions that follow.

CHIEF NEGOTIATOR. State or national unions provide individuals with collective bargaining training and experience to assist local unions in the bargaining process. Often bargaining is the primary work activity for those individuals, and their approach to bargaining can have a significant impact on your negotiations. Some unions rely heavily on "business agents" who are usually elected officers of the union organization with more authority than members of the local union. However, outside business agents may not have as much familiarity with local issues, and in some cases, depending on their experience, with public sector bargaining procedures as well. Many governing bodies will also engage a bargaining professional, usually an experienced labor attorney, to assist its bargaining team in the preparation for and conduct of bargaining. Those individuals leading each of the respective negotiating teams will be referred to as the "chief negotiator" for their respective teams.

BARGAINING TEAM. Most collective bargaining agreements will define the process for the negotiation of a successor agreement when the current agreement approaches expiration. That process will, generally, include a provision for negotiations between "bargaining teams" representing the labor and management sides. The bargaining teams usually include a defined number of individuals: management employees on the management side and employees who are members of the bargaining unit on the labor side. Five team members per side is not uncommon. Each side selects its own team members. On the labor side, team members other than the chief negotiator usually include senior bargaining unit members. Others with particular knowledge of issues to be bargained may be called to serve on the team as well. You can usually expect to find the local union president as one of the members of the union's bargaining team.

Next, we will begin the walk through the bargaining process from beginning to end and describe what goes on at each stage. This includes a healthy dose of "what to do" and, likewise, "what not to do." While I can't guarantee that you won't make mistakes even after reading and applying the information to follow, I can guarantee a fuller understanding of the process and the ability to avoid some of the more common mistakes. Let's begin with a review of some of the unique attributes of public sector bargaining and talk a little about why it's different from collective bargaining in the private sector.

CHAPTER 2

Public vs. Private Sector Bargaining

Public sector collective bargaining is fundamentally different from private sector bargaining because the employment relationship between public- and private-sector employees is different. Those differences limit both public sector labor and management in the kinds of issues they can bring to the bargaining table and the scope of benefits they can hope to attain. These limitations are often frustrating for public sector governing board members, many of whom work in the private sector, when they are forced to deal with the legal restraints imposed on the public sector bargaining process. The following will review some of those differences while recognizing, however, that state law requirements vary from state to state.

In essence, there are three reasons for the differences between public- and private-sector bargaining. First, the statutes that create and govern the operation of the public sector enterprise limit the scope of its authority. Second, because it is an agency of government, whether local, city, or state, the actions of the public sector enterprise are "state action" and must not violate the constitutional rights of either the public in general or its public employees. And third, because the public sector enterprise has little if any direct control of its funding and must operate within budgetary constraints imposed by others.

We begin with the notion that the public entity exists because laws have been passed causing it to exist. Those laws also impose statutory purposes to fulfill, whether educating our children, plowing snow on the roads, or performing some other governmental function. Members of the governing body must accept the fact that its primary mandate is to deliver the services that the enterprise was created to provide. It simply can't "close the doors" and go out of business or move the enterprise to another state, as can occur in the private sector.

Additionally, the processes by which the enterprise employs its personnel are often governed by a complex statutory scheme that has often been in place since pre-collective bargaining times. For example, Ohio, like other states, defines by law the criteria necessary for licensure to teach in public schools. There simply is no option to override those criteria by a bargaining agreement. Likewise, school bus drivers, boiler operators, firefighters, and numerous other public sector jobs have some form of certification or licensure as a condition of employment.

One of the critical distinctions is the difference between the requirements necessary to *create* a public sector employer/ employee relationship (getting hired) and the requirements that apply *after the relationship has been created*. In many cases, post-hiring provisions are also defined by statute. Looking back to our teaching example, statutory benefit provisions that apply during public school teacher employment include such benefits as the accrual and use of sick leave and minimum salary levels. These benefits can be and often are the subject of labor negotiations that almost always result in contracted increases above the statutory benefit levels. As a result, the statutory provisions become a "benefit floor" and contract negotiations focus on benefits above, or in addition to the statutory floor. Bargaining issues that relate to the "wages, hours, and terms and conditions of employment" are fair game in the bargaining process.[1]

At the same time, some significant issues are simply taken off the table by state law and are not available for negotiations. One example is the issue of retirement benefits for public employees in Ohio. Those benefits are provided by state retirement agencies and are not available for negotiations.[2] This is not the case in some other states, and it's fair to say that the negotiation of retirement benefits for public employees can add a large dimension of both complexity and cost to the process.

In some states it may also be possible to supersede some provisions of state law through a collective bargaining agreement. Tread carefully here, as the mere mention of an issue in the agreement that is also subject to state law may not be sufficient to trump that state law provision. If your goal is to supersede state law with a bargaining agreement provision, make sure that you include all of the necessary language to accomplish that result. Consult your legal counsel on that issue before attempting to supersede any provision of state law.

Employment rights defined by federal law are, as a general matter, also not subject to limitation or change by collective bargaining except in those narrow instances where the federal statute gives leeway to local labor agreements. Although the myriad federal laws and regulations governing employment often apply to both the public and private sectors, they represent a different set of rules that exist regardless of any bargaining agreement. Be careful to avoid entering into a bargaining agreement that conflicts with legal requirements that you can't supersede. Being stuck between complying with its labor agreement or a conflicting provision of law is a very difficult problem for the enterprise and one to be avoided in the bargaining process.

As noted above, the actions of public employers at nearly every level constitute "state action," making them potentially liable for the violation of the federal constitutional rights of public employees, as well as members of the public in general.[3] Private employers, on the other hand, are free to regulate their employees as needed, so long as they don't violate existing employment laws. This distinction recently came to the fore in the United States Supreme Court decision in *Janus v. American Federation of State, County, and Municipal Employees, Council 31, ET Al.*[4] In Part II we will discuss the *Janus* decision in some detail, but for now it will suffice to say that the decision struck down the long-established practice in many states of permitting "agency fee" payments to unions to be deducted from the wages of employees who chose not to join the union but who had the benefit of union representation. The basis for the decision was the court's determination that agency fee payments violated the First Amendment rights of the employees who had chosen not to join the union or to otherwise support its activities. The constitutional rights of public employees can manifest in numerous circumstances in the workplace and, like many other public employee issues, cannot be limited by collective bargaining.

Public sector economics represents the ultimate distinction between public and private sector bargaining. In the private sector, an increase in the cost of labor may, depending on competition and market conditions, be offset by an increase in the price of the product. On the other hand, tax-supported enterprises have little control over the extent of tax revenue available for salary and benefits. Thus, the fund of dollars available for that purpose is both limited and, as a practical matter, beyond the ability of management to readily change. A full understanding of these limitations is critical for both sides. There simply is no money tree in the backyard.

Management, likewise, must enter the process understanding that it is limited by law in its dealings with its employees and, generally, can't effectively use the bargaining process to change that. For example, in some states the process for terminating public employees, a common management issue, is defined by law and may not be changed by union contract. Knowing the limitations that will apply to your contract and establishing reasonable expectations on both sides about what they can and cannot hope to achieve in bargaining is an important part of the process.

For those whose goal in public sector collective bargaining is to "run it like a business," the process will be frustrating indeed. It's simply not a business, and bargaining can't change that fact.

Now that we've explored some of the limitations of public sector bargaining, let's take a look at the types of processes available and consider which one might work best for your enterprise.

CHAPTER 3

Flavors of Bargaining

The mention of collective bargaining often conjures images of smoke-filled rooms with gruff, heavy-set union types on one side of the table and well-dressed, slick-haired management types on the other side, with the union negotiator loudly making demands and the management equally loudly saying "no" to those demands. While that scenario can, and often does, still take place (minus the smoke-filled room), newer developments have brought a lot of options to the bargaining process. The following will refer, generally, to the "smoke-filled room" image as "traditional bargaining" and to the newer range of options as "interest-based bargaining." However, there are a wide range of options between those general categories.

TRADITIONAL BARGAINING

Let's begin with traditional bargaining. This is the historical labor negotiations format, characterized by the making of demands by each side followed by discussions (sometimes) and counterproposals. Each demand is presented in writing and requires a response, also in writing. Discussions are generally engaged in only by the union's chief negotiator on the labor side and the chief negotiator on the management side. While each side's bargaining teams are present, team members other than the chief negotiator seldom speak in bargaining sessions unless their comments are privately orchestrated in advance.

Traditional bargaining requires a response to each proposal in writing, and generally, no agreement is ever reached on any proposal without some concession from the other side. The concession may not directly relate to the proposal, but it is nonetheless a concession on some bargaining issue. As you can imagine, traditional bargaining leads to large numbers of proposals, some of which represent genuine problems to be resolved, while others are there simply as "cannon fodder" to leverage the bargaining position of the side making the proposals.

The initial challenge for management in traditional bargaining is to determine which of the union's proposals really matter and which are simply there for leverage and can be disposed of easily. This usually requires a great deal of discussion, with questions like, "what is the problem that you are trying to solve with this proposal?" Some unions will decline to even engage in such discussions, responding simply that "we asked for it because we want it," leaving management to speculate as to which of the union's many proposals really matters to them. Some union chief negotiators bring drama to the bargaining table as demonstrated by verbal attacks on the management side's bargainers, ripping up written responses to union proposals, and overturning furniture. Fortunately, these behaviors have become less common over time.

The traditional process is confrontational, time-consuming, and inefficient. It can easily lead to a collapse of the bargaining process and strikes. The contracts that result from the traditional process can leave both sides unhappy and create acrimony that infects the working relationships between labor and management through the term of the contract.

INTEREST-BASED BARGAINING

Recognizing the limitations of the traditional bargaining process, representatives of the Federal Mediation and Conciliation Service (FMCS) developed some alternatives that offer a radically different approach.[1] It is described, generally, as "Interest-Based Bargaining" (IBB) and differs from the traditional approach in a number of ways.

First, rather than a test of strength as represented by traditional bargaining, IBB is a problem-solving exercise designed to address issues that impact both sides of the process. The IBB process does this by having each side identify its *interests* in the issue being bargained, in a joint search for a solution that serves the interests of both sides. For example, assume that the union has proposed an across-the-board increase in the number of paid sick leave days for the members of the bargaining unit. The union's "interest" is in obtaining the additional benefit for its members. However, the management side can point to (1) increased labor cost, (2) the potential for increased sick leave usage, and (3) difficulties in finding substitutes, thus impairing its ability to provide essential services. Each side has interests in the proposal. The IBB process focuses on those interests rather than simply limiting discussions to the union's demand.

IBB is a problem-solving process, and the first goal is to identify the problem to be solved. When discussions in our example lead to the conclusion that the current sick leave benefit is at least as good as that of similar enterprises and that few employees use the full allocation under the current contract, it is easy to conclude that there is no real problem to be resolved, in which case the proposal is never made, or if made, withdrawn. In other cases, the discussions may lead to creative problem-solving solutions that benefit both sides.

The IBB process involves a number of preliminary steps. The first step, training, is usually conducted by an FMCS mediator and includes members of both labor and management teams at the same time. Training is essential for both sides, since the IBB process is so radically different from the traditional bargaining model that many of the bargainers have used in the past. The most important aspect of the training is to bring all of the participants to an understanding of the difference between an "interest" and a "proposal." Once understood, each side can begin to plan its negotiations agenda with the goal of identifying genuine problems to be solved.

What's an interest? In IBB bargaining, an interest is a benefit to either the labor or management side of the bargaining. In our paid sick leave example above, labor has an interest in obtaining additional amounts of paid leave for its members. However, as noted, it's not a shared interest because it does not benefit management. IBB bargaining looks for the shared interest, the "win-win" solution to the problem. Shared interests are those that benefit both the side proposing the interest as well as the other side. Here are a couple of examples. A governing board member proposes an "interest" in having employees agree to a 10% pay cut. Taxpayer money is saved, the enterprise operates well within budget and all is well. But, is that a genuine interest? Let's further assume that our board member gets what he or she wants. Now the employees are paid less than the market value of their services and will leave for other jobs. Replacements are hard to hire because new employees don't want to work for lower wages. Existing employees are forced to do more work for less pay, and morale is in the dumps. What appeared to be a genuine interest to our board member may not work out in reality. It was not an interest because there was no mutual benefit to be gained from it.

Likewise, the employee who argues for a 10% pay increase when current pay levels are competitive in the market may also have not correctly identified a true interest. Let's assume that management agreed to the pay raise, which it couldn't afford in the first place, only to discover that it now has a serious budget shortfall. Employee layoffs follow, and the employee who argued hardest for the pay increase "interest" finds himself out of work. Each of these examples highlights the fact that the identification of a true "interest" for IBB purposes should consider both how it will benefit the union and how it will benefit the enterprise.

Another appealing aspect of the IBB process is the limitation of issues. This is difficult, especially for union bargain teams that have traditionally loaded their bargaining packages with lots of proposals in hopes of gaining an advantage from the sheer weight of their package. Yet, the promise of IBB is to attain solutions to real problems—and to do it without the protracted dance that often permeates traditional bargaining. It is not uncommon for parties to agree to limit each side's issues to no more than ten, excluding wages and insurance. Such a limitation requires a true commitment to the IBB process and is a good indicator of the willingness of each side to fully participate.

Remember the traditional bargaining "gag" on all of the team members except for the chief negotiator? Well, the IBB process encourages *all of the members* of each team to speak, so long as the comments are directed at solving the problem. Rather than acrimonious exchanges, bargaining discussions become problem-solving exercises involving all of the members of each bargaining team. Here's an example: In a private sector negotiating session, management proposes a wage reduction in a particular department and cites low productivity as the reason. Discussions directed at the productivity issue result in suggestions such as (1) replace existing outdated equipment and (2) change work rules to permit more effective use of the workforce in the department. In the end, management got what it really wanted—increased productivity—while labor avoided a pay cut. This kind of "win-win" solution is the goal of the IBB process.

The IBB process generally requires the use of a facilitator, and that role often falls to the local FMCS representative. The facilitator will have conducted a joint pre-bargaining training session and, during the actual bargaining, will oversee the IBB process to ensure that all parties are playing by the rules and that discussions are moving toward a successful conclusion. Team members who have traditional bargaining experience will often tend to lapse back to the traditional model and try to engage in positional bargaining within the IBB process. That sort of behavior will be discouraged by the facilitator. Both in planning and execution, it's essential that both negotiating teams follow the same bargaining model at the same time. For one side to negotiate within the IBB model while the other is negotiating in the traditional bargaining model is a guarantee of failure.

While the IBB process is very useful in getting quickly to the real issues in bargaining, there are a few areas where it doesn't function quite so well. Foremost among these are the direct monetary benefit issues, including wages, salary, insurance, and other monetary benefit issues. While employee compensation may be viewed as a "problem," in reality the resolution of those issues routinely devolves to something that looks much more like traditional bargaining, with the union demanding one level of increase and management responding with a far different proposal. We will discuss the mechanics of dealing with this in more detail later. Suffice to say here that even IBB, as appealing as it may sound, is not an easy answer to all of the potential bargaining issues.

IBB bargaining offers many advantages for both labor and management. The experience of mutual problem-solving opens the door for continued dialogue during the resulting contract and offers the potential for avoiding many disputes that could otherwise result in grievances. Likewise, the focus on genuine problem-solving and limitation of issues generally shortens the time frame for bargaining. It is not uncommon to reach an agreement in a day of IBB bargaining while the same teams, using the traditional model, could spend a week or more trying to reach the same agreement.

HYBRID MODELS

A third option is the use of a combination or "hybrid" approach. In this model, issues that can realistically be characterized as "problem-solving" issues are designated for IBB bargaining, with others, usually including salary and monetary benefit issues, dealt with in the traditional model. All of this is done by agreement, in advance of the actual bargaining sessions. There are many nuances of the IBB process, all of which have worked in particular circumstances, and bargaining teams can always exercise their own creativity to design enhancements that work for them. One variation that I have used successfully involves the use of a time schedule, with each issue limited to a pre-set time limit for discussion and resolution. In addition, bargaining teams are divided into two different groups, with each group given a separate set of issues and schedules. The divided groups then report their recommendations to the combined bargaining teams for either approval, which is generally the case, or rejection.

Choosing a Bargaining Flavor

It's important to select a bargaining style that best fits the circumstances of the forthcoming negotiations. Mature contracts, here used to mean those that have been renegotiated at least twice, as opposed to initial contracts or newly implemented contracts, are best suited for the IBB process. However, if the labor/management relations during the course of the contract have been rocky, filled with discord and, perhaps, multiple grievances, or if the bargaining goals of management are such as to involve likely "strike issues" on the labor side, IBB may not be right for your negotiations.

IBB bargaining requires agreement of both sides to engage in that process. Usually this is discussed during the planning process. If there is no agreement, the default is usually traditional bargaining. However, if the existing collective bargaining agreement specifies a bargaining style or specific bargaining process, the specified process will be used—unless both sides can agree otherwise. Union teams are often reluctant to make the transition from traditional bargaining to IBB simply because it's fundamentally different from the style they're used to. I've often suggested that the teams undergo IBB training first, and then decide if they're willing to commit to the IBB process. In most cases that commitment is much easier after both teams have had a good look at the IBB process. As noted below, agreement on the bargaining style to be followed in negotiations, as much in advance as possible, is essential to successful negotiations.

Having now had a look at the available "flavors of bargaining," it's time to roll up our sleeves and get ready for the actual bargaining. But, like so much in life, the key to success lies in the planning, which is what we will talk about next.

CHAPTER 4

Preparing to Bargain

As in many life endeavors, preparation is the key to success. Here we will review the process of getting ready to bargain: how to build your bargaining team, what issues to prepare for, and when to interact with the opposing side as part of the planning process. If your enterprise has a bargaining agreement currently in effect, you should start there. Most collective bargaining agreements will include a process and timeline for the bargaining of a successor agreement. Preparation, however, should begin well before the actual bargaining process. As you review the following, keep in mind that even bargaining preparation will be affected by the bargaining style to be used, and adjustments may need to be made depending on the style ultimately chosen for bargaining.

PREPARATION STRATEGIES

Many bargaining agreements will address such matters as when bargaining must commence, who, if anyone, must initiate the bargaining process and the manner in which it should be initiated, the size of the bargaining teams for each side, and details regarding the submission of and response to bargaining proposals. Accordingly, it is a good idea to begin with a review of the current agreement's bargaining provisions. Absent an agreement by the parties to do otherwise, the bargaining provisions in the current agreement will control the process. After the review, sketch out a timeline, leaving ample time for preparation by your team.

Preparation is vastly different if your union is newly certified and seeking to bargain its first contract. Here, you have no existing agreement and no bargaining history for guidance. Most likely state law will govern the initial bargaining process, and you should look to your legal counsel for guidance on the procedural issues and timeline. Beyond that, you should also look to negotiated agreements between other public sector employers in your area and bargaining units containing similar groups of employees as those included in your new union for guidance. Also consider the promises made by the union in its organizing campaign; many of them will certainly make their way into the bargaining process.

Bargaining Teams

As noted earlier, most collective bargaining agreements will address the number of individuals who can participate on each side's bargaining team. Five is a fairly common team member number, but that can vary. Sometimes additional folks can take part in the process as "observers" who can be in the room but who cannot speak. Most bargaining sessions are conducted in private and are attended only by designated members of the union, for the labor side, and managers, for the management side. In most cases, the union side will also include a bargaining professional who will serve as the union's chief negotiator. Likewise, management will, as discussed later, likely want legal counsel on its team as well.

Bargaining style should be one of the first considerations in selecting your team. If bargaining has, in the past, bargained in the traditional bargaining model, some of the team members may have difficulty adjusting to the IBB "brainstorming" process. On the other hand, those experienced in IBB bargaining can become easily frustrated when operating in the traditional mode. This is another reason to determine bargaining style as early in the process as possible.

SELECTING YOUR CHIEF NEGOTIATOR

In my view, the most important part of building a management bargaining team is the selection of legal counsel to lead that team as chief negotiator. Let us begin with some of the reasons why counsel is necessary in the first place.

Some managers—for example, new school superintendents eager to win the favor of their governing boards—will boast that they "know all about it" and claim that counsel is an unnecessary expense. History has proven, time and time again, the folly of that claim. Look at it this way: your labor contract defines the employer's obligations to its employees. Yet, at the same time, volumes of federal and state law *also* define those obligations. In some (very limited) circumstances, the state law requirements may be superseded by the contract, but those are exceptions, not rules. However, the federal provisions cannot be superseded unless expressly provided in the legislation. A labor agreement in conflict with the requirements of federal or state law puts the employer between the proverbial "rock and a hard place" because it cannot satisfy both. Legal counsel can identify and help avoid those conflicts.

Another reason to employ counsel is to help navigate the shoals of coming developments in state law. Not to suggest that counsel comes equipped with a crystal ball, but to suggest that counsel representing, for example, public school districts, is far more likely to be aware of trends than those spending their time immersed in the day-to-day operations of the enterprise. Experienced legal counsel will also be familiar with how labor arbitrators approach contract interpretation when resolving grievance arbitration disputes, and can provide insight on drafting provisions that are more likely to withstand challenge if a grievance is filed.

Finally, legal counsel who bargains as part of his or her practice will likely have seen many of the union's proposals in other contexts and may also have experience with the union's bargaining representative. A good working relationship between the union's and the board's chief negotiators is a strong asset in the bargaining process. On the other hand, an acrimonious relationship can work the other way.

Experienced counsel who is familiar with the bargaining style you intend to use, familiar with the union's chief bargaining representative, familiar with the issues likely to arise, and knowledgeable about the state and federal laws governing the operation of your enterprise is a valuable asset in the bargaining process. Select that individual with care and listen carefully to what he or she has to say. If your enterprise belongs to a statewide organization such as a "school boards association" or a "township trustees association," the association can be a good source for information about individuals qualified to serve as chief negotiators. Likewise, check with similar public sector employers in your area who have recently completed bargaining, as they may also have good referral information.

PICKING YOUR TEAM MEMBERS

As a general matter, each side of the bargaining process has the right to select the members of its bargaining team, the only limitation being that team members must be members of the side represented by that team. For example, the union's team is made up of members of the bargaining unit represented by the union; the management team is made up of administrators, supervisors, or governing board members. The chief negotiators are usually the only outsiders permitted on the team. The actual selection is usually made by the bargaining committee (for the union) and the manager in charge of the bargaining process (for management).

Getting the right personalities on your bargaining team is also an important step in the process. As noted earlier, some personality types are better suited to the "brainstorming" aspects of IBB than others. At the same time, the experience of your bargaining unit members is also valuable, and if you have experienced managers with good working relations with the union team's membership, they should be strongly considered. Another aspect to consider is the advantage of having someone with the ability to understand and respond to the union's most likely bargaining issues.

For example, assume that one elementary school happens to have the union president as one of its teachers. A nagging issue for the elementary schools has been the school day starting time, which they want to move to a later time. When the union presents this issue in the course of bargaining, it will no doubt offer scenarios demonstrating the hardships to the elementary school's teachers resulting from the current starting time, and exaggeration sometimes happens. Having someone on the board's team who is familiar with the elementary school's operation may well dampen the urge to exaggerate the unfavorable impact aspect of the current starting time.

Another strategy is to agree in advance with the union that one of the governing body's seats on its bargaining team will be open to an administrator familiar with the issues then under discussion, and the identity of the person in that seat may change as the issues change. This gives management the ability to bring to the table individuals with specific knowledge of the day-to-day operations of proposals under discussion. A good example of this would be in the negotiations of a non-teaching school district contract involving all non-teaching employees. When issues affecting the cooks are under discussion, the manager of that department would participate on the board's bargaining team. When the issues involve bus drivers, the manager of that department would fill the "revolving" team position.

One ongoing governing board issue that can arise is whether the entire governing board or any of its members should be at the bargaining table as either team members or observers. A number of dynamics enter into this decision. For example, some board members simply do not trust the others to make the proper decision and will insist on being at the table if any board members are at the table. Having the entire board, or even a majority of its members, as part of the bargaining team presents a host of problems; for example, whether their presence constitutes a "public meeting" requiring advance public notice of each bargaining session.

There are sound reasons not to include any of the governing board members in your bargaining team. First, since the board is the ultimate decider of negotiation issues it is a lot harder to defer decisions on those issues if they, or a voting majority of them, are at the table. Think of buying a car when the salesperson, having reached the end of his or her bargaining authority, takes a break to "go talk to the boss" about your last offer. It would be impossible for the salesperson to do that if the "boss" were in the room bargaining the price of the car with you directly.

You should also expect that, if any governing board members do sit as members of the bargaining team, any comments they make will likely be taken by the union as the position of the entire governing board. This can create problems. If your bargaining team will include any member of your governing board at the table, be certain that all understand that no one member can act for the governing board because governing board decisions are made by the entire body at a duly called meeting. It is also a good practice to have board members check with the chief negotiator before taking positions at the table on issues under discussion. A union proposal that may sound good on the surface can be disastrous in operation, but the governing board member will have no way of knowing that. Yet, words of approval by one board member will often be taken by the union's bargaining team to mean that their proposal is acceptable to the entire board, and you will have a difficult time getting out of that dilemma.

My personal choice has generally been to have at least one

governing board member on the bargaining team when a governing board member is willing to commit to attending the often long and tedious bargaining sessions. Because of the importance of the labor agreement to both the governing board and the community it serves, it is essential for the governing board to fully understand what is going on in collective bargaining, and the best way to foster that understanding is for the board to have a member directly involved.

A similar decision-making process comes into play regarding the chief operating officer or superintendent. In a large enterprise, the superintendent is very much in demand and fully scheduled from morning to night. The time demands of collective bargaining simply cannot be met without doing harm to the enterprise because of the superintendent's absence. Yet, the union expects to be dealt with at the highest level and will complain that they are not viewed as being important if the superintendent does not attend all of the bargaining sessions. In an effort to minimize that problem, I have had the superintendent attend the first session and give some opening remarks about how important the bargaining process is and how he or she will be kept abreast of everything that goes on, but that he or she will simply be unable to attend many of the sessions. That said, at the very end, when the final management proposal is going to the table, the superintendent will re-enter the process, deliver that last proposal, and underscore how important it is for all to agree. Sometimes, it actually works…

You should also recognize that bargaining can be a valuable experience for your management team. Participation in collective bargaining is an important asset to administrators who have the desire to move up the management ladder. It serves both to expand their understanding of the entire operation and to give them a deeper understanding of the concerns of those on the labor side of the table. If you have such individuals, consider them as candidates for the team.

The treasurer or chief fiscal officer of your enterprise is an essential part of the negotiations process. However, that individual may have little to add to most of the more mundane issues that will come to the bargaining table, and for that reason alone, may not be a good choice for team membership. That said, it must be understood and agreed by all that the fiscal officer will be present for all finance or finance-related discussions. Most bargaining issues will cost, or save, money, and the fiscal officer should also be present for and take part in the planning discussions related to those issues.

So, as you consider building the team, other than the chief negotiator, consider the following: (1) bargaining style (traditional, IBB, or other); (2) issues likely to come to the table;[1] (3) personality and management styles of potential team members; and (4), who has worked well in past bargaining and who has not.

Finally, if the governing board, notwithstanding the cautions above, decides that its members should participate in bargaining, remember that they are the boss, and deal with it. Also, keep in mind that restrictions on the number of bargaining team members relate *only* to those individuals who are in the room, at the table, and participating in formal bargaining sessions. A great deal of work is done outside that very limited setting, where both labor and management teams are free to include anyone their respective teams would like to include.

Now that you have your bargaining team in place and have some idea of what the issues may look like, it is time to focus on developing your bargaining issues and preparing for actual bargaining.

CHAPTER 5

Developing Management Proposals

Bargaining is a two-way street. The union will come to the bargaining table with a list of demands, and management is entitled to do the same. But, in the absence of any requirement to engage in collective bargaining, management has the right to manage and control the enterprise, subject only to compliance with state and federal law.

So, you might ask, "Why should management bring proposals to the table if those proposals will limit the authority management already has?" The answer lies in the extent to which your state's bargaining law requires your enterprise to bargain. For example, if the only bargaining obligation is to negotiate "salaries and benefits," leaving your enterprise otherwise free to manage and control without union agreement, management might well want to limit its proposals to those issues related to salaries and benefits.

On the other hand, states like Ohio mandate a broad scope of bargaining that includes "wages, hours, and terms and conditions of employment," which encompasses most aspects of the labor/management relationship in the workplace.[1] The broadscale bargaining obligation forces enterprises in states like Ohio to develop bargaining proposals for desired changes in working conditions. What follows assumes that your enterprise has broadscale bargaining obligations as well as an existing negotiated agreement.[2] Developing management's issues is a critical part of the preparations process because there is, in nearly every instance, only one opportunity to bring issues to the bargaining table, and that occurs at the very beginning of the process—the first formal meeting. If management brings no proposals to the table, it is limited to responding to those brought by the union. In the traditional bargaining model, that means that management has nothing to trade except concessions.

READ YOUR CONTRACT

It's a good idea to involve your entire bargaining team in the development of management proposals, and especially so where you plan to use IBB bargaining techniques. In developing management proposals there are a large number of things to look at. I suggest you begin by reading the current contract, since that document will be the focus of the bargaining to come. If you don't understand what some of the provisions mean, ask either your chief negotiator or someone familiar with the operation of that provision. Understanding the current obligations as previously agreed to by your governing board is important as a beginning. It is also important to remember that labor contracts are not the exclusive work of either the labor or management side alone. Rather, you must assume that every word in that contract was the product of negotiation and that every obligation of either party was bought and paid for in prior negotiations. There will likely be a lot of things in the current agreement that you don't like, but remember that all of those provisions are there for a reason, and you're not writing on a clean slate.

Further, don't assume that just because there is a provision in the current contract that you don't like, that you can easily change that provision. I believe it's true that most everything in collective bargaining has a price, but that price can be quite high, and it's important to have some idea of what that price will be before you set about changing something you don't like. In that regard, the use of experienced labor counsel in planning the governing board's negotiating agenda is critical because experience will dictate how important a given provision or benefit is to the union. The more important the issue, the higher the cost of giving it up. That doesn't mean that you shouldn't take on the difficult issues, but it does mean that you should have some understanding of how difficult those issues will be before you put them on your bargaining agenda.

HISTORY LESSONS–MANAGEMENT INPUT

Preparation should also include a review of the union's proposals from the last round of negotiations. Chances are that any issue not achieved by the union in the last round will reappear in the forthcoming round of negotiations. Hopefully your management bargaining team will have kept records of prior negotiations, including both issues proposed as well as those agreed to and those withdrawn by each side.

Likewise, communication with department managers, principals, or other management-level employees regarding difficulties they may have had operating under the current agreement, and any changes they would like to see made is always helpful. In many cases managers will encourage management proposals that would simply make their jobs easier, like "Make them come to work on time." These are of no help in preparing for bargaining, but the act of reaching out to your managers does serve two valuable goals. First, it reminds them that bargaining will be happening, and it gives them an opportunity for input. Second, if bargaining doesn't go well and a strike ensues, their participation will be essential to maintaining services during the strike. They need to be involved in the process as early as possible. At the same time, avoid promising that their suggestions will make it into the management list of proposals.

Make sure that your fiscal officer also has input into the development of management's bargaining proposals. Often, seemingly mundane things become embedded into the contract that could be streamlined through the use of modern technology. Issues such as mandatory direct payroll deposit can save many thousands of dollars over the course of a contract, but the savings can't be fully realized unless direct deposit is mandatory for all members of the bargaining unit. In this instance, a simple contract change can yield substantial benefits.

Grievance History

You should also review the history of grievance activity during the term of the existing contract to determine the number of grievances filed, the specific provisions of the contract that gave rise to the grievances, and the resolution of the grievances.[3] If grievances have gone to arbitration, what was the result? Chances are, if the union lost the arbitration, it will want to change that result by changing the contract in bargaining. Ditto for management. Lots of grievances are a warning sign that labor-management relations are not as good as they might be and a signal to consider negotiating a provision for periodic labor-management meetings to discuss and resolve problems before they turn into grievances. You should also understand that the union will view a "win" in an arbitration case as affirmation that they were right and will be most reluctant to change that result. Again, it's important to know the price of what you're asking for.

SOME ISSUES YOU MAY NOT WANT TO PUT ON THE TABLE

There are potential downsides to putting certain issues on the bargaining table. For example, the union and governing board have had an ongoing disagreement about the accrual of vacation leave under the current contract. The union believes that the entire year's leave accrues at the beginning of the year, and the governing board believes that it accrues sequentially, with each payroll. Past practice is no help, as each side can point to examples confirming its belief. Each side contends that the contract language supports its position on accrual, and the union has threatened a grievance over the governing board's accrual practices. The board wants to remove the uncertainty by adding language to the contract to confirm its view of when accrual takes place. While a contractual clarification would remove the uncertainty, remember that the union would consider such a "clarification" as a concession, giving up a benefit that it believes it already has. Such a concession will not be easily achieved and will come with a hefty cost, if it can be achieved at all.

Here's the problem. If the board brings its clarification to the table as a bargaining proposal and fails to get agreement, the union will eventually file its grievance and, when the board asserts its belief that the contract justifies its accrual practice, the union will, quite rightly, point out that the board tried—and failed—to negotiate the language that it now, in the grievance, asserts is already clear. In this example, the proposal made and later dropped can come back to haunt the board.

The negative consequences in this example could be avoided by an agreement to the effect that the withdrawal of the board's proposal will be made "as if never proposed," so that it can't later be used against the board. However, many bargainers fail to fully understand the consequences of a failed proposal and simply withdraw the proposal when it becomes clear that agreement is impossible.

The above is but one example of the sort of caution that should accompany the development of management's bargaining proposals. The best advice is for management to avoid proposals giving it the right to do that which it already has the authority to do without the proposal. When developing management proposals, consider both the overall benefit to the enterprise if the proposal were to be achieved as well as the cost of getting the union's team to agree to it. As we said before, everything has a price, and it's far better to have some idea of what that price is before putting the proposal on the table than to find out later that the ultimate price of success is one that the governing board is unwilling to pay.

MANDATORY AND PERMISSIVE
SUBJECTS OF BARGAINING

In most cases, state law provides the legal framework for public
sector collective bargaining, and it will also define what must be
bargained about. These are referred to as mandatory subjects of
bargaining. Mandatory subjects of bargaining are those required
by law and about which good-faith bargaining cannot be lawfully refused by either side. In Ohio, for example, mandatory
subjects of bargaining are wages, hours, and terms and conditions of employment, as well as any provision of an existing collective bargaining agreement.[4] This means that a new provision
added to the bargaining agreement becomes, thereafter, a mandatory subject of bargaining for all future negotiations, so long
as it remains in the agreement. This is true even if the subject of
the provision would otherwise have been permissive. State law
provisions vary widely in this area, and your circumstances may
be different.

Permissive subjects of bargaining are those that either
side can legitimately refuse to bargain because they are too far
outside the scope of the employment relationship to be considered mandatory. For example, a teacher's union proposal to
the effect that all school children will come to school wearing
clean clothes may well be beneficial, but it is also beyond the
scope of the employer's ability to guarantee. Permissive subjects of bargaining can be proposed and even discussed, but
cannot be continued to impasse, a term we will discuss in more
detail later.[5]

MANAGEMENT RIGHTS

In light of our earlier discussion about broad-scope bargaining obligations, you might well be asking why we even bother to mention management rights. The answer is that most every state recognizes and preserves some level of management rights in the public sector, and care should be taken to not bargain those rights away, either intentionally or inadvertently. Ohio, for example, while mandating broad-scope negotiations, also articulates in law a broad panoply of management rights that exist "…unless a public employer agrees otherwise in a collective bargaining agreement."[6] Care should be taken not to offer, or agree to, proposals that can result in a diminution of management rights. For example, management has the right to determine the starting and ending time of the workday for members of the bargaining unit. But, once starting times are included in the bargaining agreement, it is no longer within the discretion of management to change at will.[7] So, our building principal who wanted the board to change the labor contract to "make them come to work on time" is actually encouraging an unwise course of action by management, since the right to direct employees to report to work on time is a management right that should not be negotiated. Be careful what you ask for, you might just get it.[8]

UNDERSTANDING THE COST

While collective bargaining can cover a wide range of issues, wages and monetary benefits are sure to be there. Addressing these issues requires a lot of preparation to be ready to deal with proposals

for increases in wages and benefits. This means the ability to reasonably and accurately estimate the cost of the union's salary and
benefit proposals, independently from what the union may say
they will cost, and the ability to project the revenue available to
pay for such proposals.

Unlike the private sector, most of the enterprise's income and
expense information is contained in public records obtainable by
the union's negotiators. They will know, for example, the size of
the carryover balance, as well as any projected increase in funding
for the projected period of the contract. But public funding is
complex and often extremely difficult to project into the future.
Tax revenue depends on tax collection, and revenues tend to drop
in times of recession. Additional tax revenue is often beyond the
control of the governing board and can't be counted on until the
tax is actually approved, levied, and collected. Likewise, committed expenses are also difficult to predict. The cost of fuel to run
school buses, the price of health insurance, utility costs, and additional government mandates are all beyond the direct control of
the governing board but will often impact the bottom line.

Having the ability to fully understand your enterprise's
finances now and during the likely effective period of a new collective bargaining agreement is essential to your bargaining preparation. Equally important during the course of bargaining is the
ability to promptly and accurately analyze the cost of union proposals and counterproposals and to develop management counterproposals both accurately and quickly. This requires the ability
to build and use spreadsheets that will enable the management
team to quickly and accurately determine the cost of the union's
salary and benefit proposals. If your fiscal officer does not have

41

this capability, it may be necessary to recruit help from outside because you can't otherwise hope to bargain effectively.

Consider, for example, that the cost of benefits means the cost of an increase or decrease in each component of benefits under discussion. If the union proposes to increase severance pay to equal the value of all of the retiring employees' accrued and unused sick leave, what would the ultimate cost of that proposal amount to, and when would it likely be paid? In order to reasonably estimate the cost of such a proposal, you would need to know the value of sick leave currently accrued and unused by all members of the bargaining unit, the likely additional value of accrued and (expectedly) unused sick leave during the term of the contract, as well as the additional cost of any salary increases during that time. Sound complicated? It is, but doable if enough advance planning is done before bargaining. If that planning isn't done and you are trying to cost such a proposal during a bargaining session, or even between bargaining sessions, you've taken on a virtually impossible task. Planning is important, and effective planning includes developing and having access to the data and spreadsheets necessary to accurately cost union proposals.

Similar issues arise even from a more direct pay-increase proposal. For example, what would a $1 per hour pay increase for all employees cost? The answer is certainly knowable, but only if you know the aggregate number of hours likely to be worked in the course of a year as well as the number of overtime hours likely to be worked. Even then, the result of your calculations is based on assumptions that may not be correct. You can only estimate the number of employee work hours in a year based on past practice and estimates of coming needs. Yet, granting such a pay-increase proposal without having a reasonable expectation of the total cost to the enterprise and the impact of that cost on the overall operations during the contract would be irresponsible.

Employees who are paid on a salary schedule with indexed increases based on training and experience present yet another challenge for costing because the cost of the existing schedule will increase each year, even without any change in the base salary amount. Accurate cost information for bargaining requires that you know not only what an increase in the base salary would cost overall, but also that you can compare that increase to the cost of the schedule with no increase.

WATCH YOUR NEIGHBORS

Over time, similar governmental entities will tend to have similar collective bargaining agreements save for a few local differences. Thus, school district labor contracts will have very similar agreements to one another. The reason for this is twofold: first, union bargaining representatives will likely represent a number of locals in the same geographic area and will tend to encourage the same provisions from district to district. Additionally, similar entities will tend to look at what the "neighbors are doing" when planning for or responding to union proposals. Given this, it's always wise to know what similar entities in the same geographic region/economic status range are doing. This is particularly important with respect to major cost items in a collective bargaining agreement such as wages, salary schedules, health care benefits, and leave provisions. These benefits tend to establish a market price for similar labor in the area, and it is wise to know whether your enterprise's current salaries and benefits are above or below the market. Plan to make such a review a part of your negotiations planning.

PLANT SOME SEEDS – CAREFULLY

If your enterprise is faced with proposing some potentially painful salary or benefit reductions due to projected shortfalls in operating income in the forthcoming round of bargaining, you may want to "telegraph" the fiscal distress in advance. But be careful. There is a fine line between "direct dealing" with union membership, which is generally considered to be an unfair labor practice on the part of management, and letting it be known that certain issues will be very important in the forthcoming bargaining session. For example, in the times of double-digit annual increases in healthcare costs, many governing boards sought relief in the form of passing some of the cost increases on to labor. One way to sensitize the workforce to the impact of this issue was to include references in newsletters regarding cost increases and the total cost of maintaining board-paid health benefits, without, of course, any mention of the forthcoming bargaining sessions. Similarly, the inclusion of information along with pay stubs has also been used as a means of letting folks know the magnitude of cost increases (as well as the cost of the benefits they are currently receiving). On the other hand, public announcements by the governing board in advance of bargaining, such as "we are going to require employees to pay 90% of their healthcare costs" can be devastating in the long run. Such a tactic is like waving a red blanket in the face of a raging bull. The union, believing that its right to bargain such issues is being circumvented, will likely file an unfair labor practice charge for "direct dealing." Even if it doesn't, management can expect extreme resistance regarding that issue as the union is now forced to demonstrate to its membership that it can preserve the negotiated benefits it gained for them in the past from arbitrary reduction.

DON'T FORGET YOUR GOVERNING BOARD

The extent of governing board involvement in negotiations planning can cover the entire spectrum from virtually no involvement at all, giving management free rein to fashion bargaining proposals and deal with the negotiations process, to hands-on micromanagement of the process. Regardless of the inclinations of your governing board, keep in mind that they are the ones to ultimately deal with the outcome of the negotiation process. So, make sure that they are fully informed at each step of the process and that they have the opportunity for input if they wish.

Are you ready? If so, let's consider a pre-bargaining meeting with the union to chart the logistics of the forthcoming negotiations.

CHAPTER 6

Getting Ready
for Negotiations:

Pre-Bargaining Meetings, Developing
Your Proposals, and Team Training

Before IBB became a bargaining option there was little need for a pre-bargaining meeting between representatives of the union and management bargaining teams. The time and place of the first bargaining meeting was scheduled, usually by a phone call between the union president and the enterprise manager, the parties prepared their traditional bargaining proposals and showed up at the first meeting ready to bargain. The advent of IBB has brought with it the opportunity to resolve pre-bargaining issues informally, and I strongly suggest that you consider having such a meeting. There are a number of topics that can be productively addressed. First, and most important, is the bargaining style to be used in the forthcoming negotiations; whether traditional, IBB, or hybrid. Beyond that, the logistics of when and where bargaining will take place, the identification of clerical ("housekeeping") changes to the existing contract that can be easily agreed upon and, depending on the willingness of the parties, a number of other time-saving measures that could also be discussed.

Pre-bargaining meetings are informal get-togethers between the bargaining team leaders and chief negotiators on each side to address logistical and planning issues necessary to enable the formal bargaining process to go forward, to "set the table" for the actual bargaining meetings to come later. It should be made clear to all that the pre-bargaining meeting is not intended as a forum for the discussion of substantive bargaining issues. Rather, it's an *informal discussion* to address the bargaining process. Often food is involved and the meeting is very informal. Each side pays its own expenses.

BARGAINING STYLE

Bargaining style is a joint decision requiring agreement by both the union and management bargaining teams unless already specified in the existing agreement. If IBB is to be used, the mediator will require at least one joint training session for all team members, and that session should be scheduled as early as possible, as mediator schedules can become quite crowded. As noted earlier, expectations are critical. If one side believes that the IBB model will be followed and the other believes that the traditional model will be followed, problems are guaranteed. Clear expectations about what's going to happen in bargaining are essential for successful bargaining, and the pre-bargaining meeting is a good time to establish those expectations.

VENUE - COSTS

The venue for the formal collective bargaining meetings should be identified as part of the planning process and addressed in any pre-bargaining planning meetings. If space is available at the facilities of the enterprise, it is a desirable venue because the records are there, as well as copiers and computer access; and, it's free. However, some union representatives view it as a concession to negotiate on the management's premises and will demand a "neutral" site. As with other planning issues, this should be discussed and agreed on in advance of actual bargaining. I've bargained in school libraries, bus barns, and hotel basements, all with successful results. But consider that employees will want to be "on the clock" if they bargain during working hours either on- or off-site, and that you will need access to copiers, food, and computers wherever you bargain.

Off-site bargaining will involve securing space, not only for bargaining sessions but also for separate team meetings, and perhaps overnight arrangements as well. Internet access, copiers, food, and of course, coffee and tea will also be necessary. Travel time may also become a consideration. These factors sometimes also make it more difficult to maintain the confidentiality of the negotiations. There should be upfront agreement about how the costs involved in securing the facilities will be paid and, if shared, how they will be shared. Some members of the public can be quick to criticize bargaining at off-site facilities as a "paid vacation" for management and labor team members. Little do they know…

ISSUE EXCHANGE

Other important matters, such as a pre-bargaining issue exchange (which is standard practice in IBB bargaining but not always used in traditional bargaining) should be discussed. In addition, the identification of non-controversial, "housekeeping" contract changes, such as the correction of typographical errors or clarification of existing contract language (so long as both sides agree on the intent) is also a relevant pre-bargaining topic. Sometimes a subcommittee consisting of two members of each bargaining team can review the contract and list provisions needing clarification as well as suggestions for that clarification. The agreed recommendations will then be addressed at the initial bargaining meeting.

The form in which proposals will be presented is also fair game for discussion in a pre-bargaining meeting.[1] Other issues that may require enormous amounts of time in actual bargaining can sometimes be identified and addressed in other, more productive ways. One example of this is the negotiation of supplemental contracts for schoolteachers: such things as athletic coaching positions, yearbook advisor, and the like can add up to hundreds of contracts issued each year. The renegotiation of each of those contracts separately could consume the bargaining teams for years, but a separate committee made up of both labor and management members can make informed recommendations that would shorten the actual bargaining process significantly. An informal process to put such a committee in place can be developed in a pre-bargaining meeting.

Pre-bargaining meetings can also set the tone for what's to follow, and in a mature bargaining relationship serve to enhance and shorten the formal bargaining process. In addition to the agenda items, the meeting may give some insight into the individuals who will be serving on each side's bargaining teams as well as the major issues that each side wishes to address. A great deal of information can be learned simply by knowing who will be on the other side's bargaining team. For example, if a non-teaching school bargaining unit has loaded its team with bus drivers, it's a good bet that there will be a lot of bus driver issues arriving at the bargaining table.

FINANCIAL INFORMATION

Another significant issue that can be addressed at a pre-bargaining meeting is the identification of financial or other data that will be critical to the bargaining process. Unlike the private sector, most of the information related to the enterprise's operations and finances is public data, available for the asking. The enterprise has no secrets to keep regarding its income and expenses, and having both sides working from a common set of basic facts can avoid a great deal of unnecessary angst in bargaining. Yet, if the labor side believes that there is a great deal more money available for salaries and benefits than that supported by the factual data, the seeds of discord can easily grow. Agreement on basic facts is important, and the pre-bargaining meeting is a good opportunity to begin establishing those facts. Effective bargaining is driven by facts, not speculation, and the sooner the relevant facts are determined and accepted by both sides, the better the chances for a successful resolution of the bargaining process.

If both sides are willing, the pre-bargaining meeting is also a good opportunity to establish an agenda of issues to be addressed and the length of each bargaining session.[2] I personally like to schedule ending times as well as starting times in traditional bargaining. If substantial progress is being made, the parties can always agree to continue the session beyond the scheduled ending time. If not, an ending time provides a legitimate reason to continue the discussions to another time. Remember, it's important for both sides to be on the same page regarding what's expected of them.

IBB TRAINING

Training is a critical part of the IBB process, and your mediator will most likely require that all bargaining team members take part in IBB training prior to the commencement of formal negotiations. This, too, is a pre-bargaining informal meeting for the purpose of familiarizing the team members with the IBB process and getting them ready to use it effectively. If the union and management have engaged in IBB bargaining before, the decision is usually pretty easy, especially if they feel that their interests have been well served by the process. Most bargaining teams that have experienced IBB never return to the traditional bargaining model. However, there is no guarantee, and the question needs to be addressed for each round of contract negotiations. If either team believes that IBB didn't work well for them, they will likely not be willing to do it again. If either of the teams is unwilling to try IBB because they are unfamiliar with the process, the best course may be for both bargaining teams to participate in IBB training with the federal mediator who can explain the process, answer questions, and permit both sides to make an informed decision. After they've had a good look at IBB many will decide to give it a try. If both sides don't agree to the IBB process, traditional bargaining is the default. Often compromise can be reached by identifying some issues to be addressed in the IBB process and others in the more traditional mode (hybrid bargaining).

WHAT IS AN "INTEREST"?

IBB training is focused on getting both sides to distinguish between "interests," which are the focus of IBB, and "proposals," which represent the focus of traditional bargaining. Additionally, the concept of brainstorming during the collective bargaining process requires a lot of adjustment for many participants, especially those who have participated in traditional bargaining in the past. Training for IBB teams usually takes several hours. One of the benefits is that the team members will get to know each other, as well as the mediator.

The key here is understanding the difference between an "interest" and a proposal. Here's an example. Suppose that additional vacation leave is what the union wants. In traditional bargaining, the initial proposal might look something like "Management shall provide not less than forty paid vacation days per year for each member of the bargaining unit." In IBB bargaining, on the other hand, the interest might look more like, "How can bargaining unit members achieve additional paid annual vacation leave?" The goal is similar, but the presentation is substantially different. Rather than listing demands, the training will focus on identifying real problems and identifying the interests of each side and different possible resolutions to those problems. After the IBB training, each side will develop its interests for discussion in bargaining. Those interests are then exchanged with the other side, usually at another informal meeting (the issue exchange meeting).

Pre-Bargaining Issue Exchange – IBB

A meeting for the exchange of interests is a part of the IBB bargaining process, but it is not intended for bargaining itself. Rather, the purpose is to exchange and focus on the interests that each side wishes to explore during the formal bargaining sessions. The exchange of interests usually takes place at a joint meeting facilitated by the mediator and can take from a few minutes to several hours. The meeting usually also involves a discussion of the information, especially financial information necessary to consider and resolve the interests presented. The production of information is usually assigned to the side having access to that information but, during actual bargaining, either side will have difficulty if it can't produce facts to support the "problem" it wants to resolve through bargaining. The mediator may ask questions about the nature of the problem that caused a particular interest to come to the bargaining table in an effort to further focus on the problem and to identify the information necessary to resolve it. The interests brought forward by each side during the issue exchange meeting define the parameters of the forthcoming negotiations; no additional issues will be permitted after that time.

Unlike traditional bargaining where all of the talking is done by each side's chief negotiator, the IBB process places the presentation of interests on individual team members. Thus, for example, an interest related to the operation of the middle school might be presented by the middle school principal, while an interest related to the timing of payroll might be presented by the chief fiscal officer. If an interest requires technical information to enable the team to address it in bargaining, an individual who is not a member of the bargaining team could be scheduled to provide that information during the course of the formal bargaining meeting.

The role of the chief negotiator is vastly changed in IBB. Individual bargaining team members, rather than the chief negotiator, will be expected to present their assigned interests both at the exchange meeting and in the formal bargaining setting to follow.

Pre-Bargaining Issue Exchange – Traditional

A pre-bargaining issue exchange is also beneficial when the parties are following the traditional bargaining model. It is helpful to both sides to get a preview of what the other side wants from bargaining as early as possible. Like the IBB bargaining, the traditional issue exchange should not be confused with a formal bargaining session. Arguments about the merits of a particular issue being brought forward should be saved for the formal bargaining sessions. The issue exchange also gives each team a chance to get a look at the other side and have a chance to weigh the different personalities on the opposing bargaining team. It also provides a chance to ask questions about the other side's proposals and attempt to focus on the underlying problem. What is presented on paper as a bargaining demand is often far from the actual goal behind the proposal, and the sooner the true objective can be determined, the better. As in the case of an IBB exchange, the identification of information necessary to the bargaining process should be a part of the exchange, and a plan for sharing that information with both sides should be developed. Additionally, if an informal pre-bargaining meeting does not happen, the issue exchange will provide the opportunity to discuss all of the agenda items that would have been covered at that meeting.

MANAGEMENT TEAM PLANNING AND PREPARATION

Although the following refers to "management team," the discussion is equally applicable to the union's bargaining team. The key is preparation for the actual bargaining to come. After your pre-bargaining meeting and issue exchange, the real work of getting ready to bargain can begin. However, that work will differ depending on the bargaining style chosen by the parties. Let's talk first about IBB preparation. Remember that IBB is an "interest-based" problem-solving exercise. During bargaining, the mediator will ask the side proposing the interest to state the problem they are trying to solve and list the team's interest in that resolution. Here's an example: suppose a teachers' union proposes an interest in adding additional personal leave days to the contract.[3] The teacher/team member selected by the team to speak for that specific proposal might then point to the interest in recruiting and retaining qualified staff through a competitive benefit package, the personal benefit of having a right to paid time off, and similar beneficial interests for teachers. The mediator will list these on the board and then ask the management side for its interests in the personal leave proposal. Management will point to its interest in maintaining control of its budget, noting that each paid leave day for the entire teaching staff costs $ xxxx. Management might also note its interest in maintaining operations, which could be seriously harmed if a large percentage of the teaching staff decides to all use a paid leave day at the same time, as well as the fact that most of the current personal leave already in the contract goes unused. As in the case of the union, the management team will have designated a specific team member to address this proposal, and that individual will be prepared to articulate the management's interests. Consider, though, that unless management's interests are identified and made part of the discussion, leaving only the union's interests for consideration, management will have a much more difficult time resolving the issue without costly concessions. That's why bargaining team training is so important.

Your team members need to spend some time together considering the possible outcomes of each of the "interest" proposals advanced by the union and whether or not any of those potential outcomes could be an acceptable solution. If there are no acceptable outcomes, management should be prepared to point out that either: (1) there is no real problem to be solved or, (2) the proposed solution violates a significant management interest. Agreement to maintain "current contract language" is a way to resolve issues for which there is no acceptable change. Often, though, good planning will lead to creative solutions that address the interest of both sides—which is exactly what IBB is intended to do.

Your team's preparation meeting should deal with both the union's proposals as well as those advanced by management. Identification of management interests should be one of the planning goals as well as consideration of possible compromises to resolve the issue. In this regard, it is very important that any governing board team members or other team members who are not familiar with the day-to-day operations of the enterprise be present at the planning meeting. It is sometimes appealing to accept a compromise proposal brought forth in actual bargaining because it sounds good when, in reality, it would pose enormous problems for management. The time to highlight those potential problems is during the team's pre-bargaining training. Team members who are assigned to speak for each of the management's "interests" should, in particular, become well versed in the nature of the problem to be discussed and the desired results. It is not uncommon for individual bargaining teams to engage in their own, private mock bargaining sessions, in preparation for IBB bargaining. It's also important for the team members to understand that legal counsel or other bargaining professionals have a much-diminished role in IBB bargaining as opposed to traditional bargaining, and it may be difficult for that individual to redirect a bargaining discussion that seems to be going off the rails. If the outside professional does all the talking, it begins to look much more like traditional bargaining, and if that's the case, it is a problem to be recognized and corrected as early as possible.[4] That's not to say that the bargaining professionals don't have a role in the process. The drafting of contract language reflecting the resolution of the interest reached by the bargaining teams is both technical and time-intensive and should be left to the professionals to do while the bargaining teams address the substantive issues.

Team training is also important in planning for traditional bargaining, though vastly different in content. In traditional bargaining, individual team members have a far less active role in the at-the-table discussions. However, each can play a significant role, especially in helping the team understand the origin, history, and nuances of the union's proposals and in helping prepare responses to them. In addition, it's always a good idea to designate one team member as the "note-taker" for the actual bargaining sessions. Session notes should be retained with the other bargaining documents as part of the record for potential use in the event of future disputes regarding what was intended by a particular provision.[5] Another reason for team preparation is to make sure the team members know when and when not to speak at the bargaining table in traditional bargaining sessions. Often a well-respected administrator known by all of the union's team can make a point far more effectively than the relative outsider leading the management's negotiations team. However, events like that should be carefully planned and scripted.

With teams built and trained, issues identified, relevant data at hand, and a contract to negotiate, it's now time to talk about the actual bargaining process. As you can see, if the pre-bargaining work is done well, actual bargaining should proceed much more smoothly.

CHAPTER 7

The Initial Bargaining Meeting

Before we launch into the bargaining process, let's quickly review how your enterprise got here and its legal obligations going forward. Your enterprise is most likely engaged in the bargaining process because state law either permits or requires it to do so and, in the past, it negotiated the contract that we are now considering for renewal. That means two things: first, that the bargaining will be done with a duly authorized union, and second, bargaining will be about workplace issues that are proper subjects for collective bargaining.[1] Assuming those conditions have been met, your obligation under state law will generally be to engage in "good-faith" bargaining in an effort to reach mutual agreement on the bargaining issues. "Good faith" is an amorphous term, the precise meaning of which may well change from state to state. For our discussion here, we will use good-faith bargaining to mean active participation in the bargaining process with the intention of reaching agreement on the contract being negotiated. Importantly, good-faith bargaining does not require agreement on any specific issue; rather, agreement should happen when the minimum requirements of each side for agreement on

61

the contract have been met. But, while the minimum requirements may not ask for very much to meet the "good-faith" standard, the overarching goal of bargaining is to reach agreement on a contract, and your efforts should be directed to that end, to the extent feasible. The first meeting will set the table for that process. Because traditional bargaining is the longer, more complex process, we will talk about it first and then review the first (and often the only) IBB meeting.

MONEY TALKS – LAST

As a general matter, wages and monetary benefits are the most important issues in any collective bargaining exercise. But experienced negotiators will nearly always defer the discussion of those issues to the end of the bargaining process, regardless of whether the bargaining is following the traditional or IBB model. The reason is simple: management views these benefits as the most important piece of the bargaining puzzle, and once the financial issues have been agreed to, it has little leverage left with which to bargain. With that in mind, it is safe to assume and plan for engaging in the discussion of the monetary issues *after* all of the non-monetary issues have been addressed.[2]

SETTING THE TONE

In the traditional bargaining model, the initial bargaining meeting sets the tone for what's to follow. Each side, primarily through their respective bargaining representatives, will create expectations by means of their proposals and choice of words as well as through body language. If the tone is demeaning, angry, and confrontational, it will be read as such by the other side. On the other hand, if the tone is friendly and open to discussion, that also will be received. Regardless of the message your team wants to send, make sure that the message is considered in advance and planned for as part of the bargaining preparation. IBB bargaining is premised on collaboration between the labor and management teams, and if you are using that model, the tone should reflect your team's willingness to collaborate. Traditional bargaining, on the other hand, can involve a wide spectrum of approaches by each side.

My personal preference is to set a friendly, non-confrontational tone, one that recognizes the right of the union's bargaining team to come to the table and make demands. The union's chief negotiator can also set a tone for bargaining. Some chief negotiators believe that they need to demonstrate their "tough" stance to their membership by taking an aggressive, demeaning approach to the management team. An aggressive response may be necessary. Here's a real-life example. During an initial bargaining session, a union's chief negotiator began by engaging in a diatribe of criticism of management, going on far longer than simple expressions of opinion would require. After about four minutes, the management team, in unison, and at my call as chief negotiator, got up and left the table. I told the union's chief negotiator that we were going into a caucus and would return when the union decided that it was there to bargain—not to lambast management.[3] After about ten minutes the union sent word that they were ready and negotiations began.

UNDERSTANDING THE UNION TEAM MEMBERS' MOTIVATION

Notwithstanding the behavior of some union negotiators, most of whom are true professionals dedicated to the welfare of their membership, it is important to keep in mind that the union's bargaining team members are employees of the enterprise. Many of them, especially those serving for the first time as bargaining team members, are more than a little reluctant to sit down as equals across the table from their employer to discuss the terms of employment. At the same time, they are told by their bargaining representative that they have the right to be there and that they should be aggressive in their demands for what they perceive to be better wages and working conditions. Others may be there out of anger and frustration with their working conditions and will demonstrate a hostile, angry approach. Regardless of the language, if the labor-side team believes that the management team is belittling their positions and refusing to take them seriously, it will, in the end, make successful bargaining a lot more difficult. While the union doesn't have the right to have their demands agreed to, it does have the right to make those demands and to have them considered by the management team.

If a collaborative tone is desired for the negotiations, the chief spokesperson for the management team should, at the earliest opportunity, recognize the union's right to be there and express appreciation for the individual employee commitments to the process. While that message may be hard to swallow for some managers, it will set a tone of collaboration at the outset.

A TRADITIONAL BARGAINING SEATING CHART

The traditional bargaining table may look quite different from the IBB table. In traditional bargaining, the focus is on each side's chief bargaining representative. The chief negotiator will usually sit at the center of the table, across from his or her counterpart on the other side. On either side of each chief negotiator will be the highest-ranking bargaining team member. For the union, this will be the local union president or bargaining chair and for the governing board, the superintendent or manager for the enterprise. Other members of each bargaining team will be seated at the same side of the table as their chief negotiator.[4]

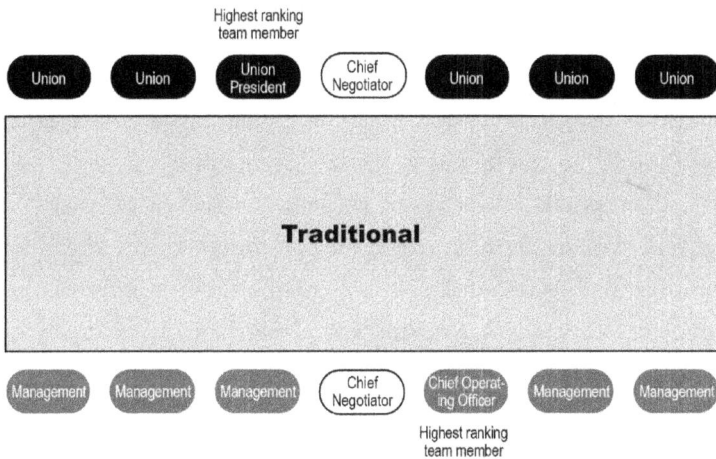

As we mentioned earlier, discussions are generally limited to the bargaining representatives only, with others only speaking when requested (or scripted) to do so. Written proposals, if not already exchanged in advance, will be exchanged by the bargaining representatives. It's customary to include a sufficient number of copies for each of the team members, and to deliver the package of proposals to the chief negotiator.

HOUSEKEEPING

Some housekeeping issues are necessary and should be addressed as early as possible in the first bargaining session. Such issues as the introduction of team members for each side and observers if any, where the bathrooms are located, what copying equipment is available (if any), and the schedule for that day's meeting, including the ending time. If caucus rooms have been reserved for each team, the location of those rooms should also be mentioned. I also like to begin the initial bargaining session by having each of the teams agree to the contract "cleanup" language that was earlier identified and recommended for agreement by both sides. Reaching an agreement at the beginning, no matter how insignificant it may be, is a good way to start negotiations.

If proposals haven't been exchanged in advance, they will generally be exchanged as one of the first things done at the initial meeting. Before responding to any of the union's proposals, it's important to spend some time reviewing them, individually, to determine exactly what end the union is trying to achieve.

"TELL ME WHAT YOU WANT, WHAT YOU REALLY, REALLY WANT."

The initial discussion at the bargaining table in traditional bargaining (or preferably, at the issue exchange) should be directed at getting a complete understanding of the other side's proposals. In short, what do they want and why do they want it? Negotiators are often not the best drafters of contract language, and the language of bargaining proposals doesn't always clearly reveal the real intent of the proposal. Thus, it falls to the other side to figure out what each proposal is *intended to* accomplish. Generally, it falls to management to figure out what the union really wants with each of its proposals. This is done through questions posed at the bargaining table, usually by the management chief negotiator. For example, "How would this change what we do now if it were agreed to?" often reveals intent. And don't forget, "What would it cost us to agree to this?" as an essential inquiry into most, if not all, of labor's proposals. Now, it's likely that the response to the cost question will be "we don't know," and that's all right. Admitting that they don't know the cost of their proposals is a concession in itself.

I'm not a fan of trying to respond to the union's demand package without first taking the time to fully review and understand the impact of those proposals with not only the management's team, but also the fiscal officer and the governing board. More about that later.

Don't Forget Management's Proposals

After you've received and reviewed the labor side's proposals, you should also be prepared to review *and explain* management's proposals. The point here is to have a legitimate reason for each of the contract changes being proposed by management. But be careful to avoid personalizing the reasons for the changes if those reasons involve specific union members. For example, suppose management wants a monetary penalty for late arrival to work, and the real reason is that Sally (who just happens to be a member of the union's bargaining team) is one of the chief offenders. If you personalize your reasons for the proposal to include Sally's misconduct, you will cause the rest of the bargaining team to rally in her defense as well as run the risk of a retaliation claim based on her participation in negotiations. It's far better to keep the reasons general and not personalize misconduct. If the union presses for examples, make sure the ones you provide do not relate to members of the union's bargaining team.

TAKING A BREAK – THE CAUCUS

The caucus is an adjournment ("time-out") of the formal bargaining session to permit each side to discuss with each other the issues that have come up at the formal bargaining table. Either side can declare a caucus, which will generally last long enough to permit discussion of the issues at hand. Some bargaining teams spend more time in caucus than they do in formal session, usually a sign of poor preparation and/or disagreement among the bargaining team members. Caucuses usually follow receipt of the other side's initial proposals and counterproposals.

Caucus is also a handy tool to defuse rising tensions and give both sides a chance for a deep breath. Negotiations can easily become emotional exercises, and little progress can be made in the heat of those emotions. The chief negotiator should be sensitive to the room "temperature" and call a caucus when necessary to cool things off.

Concluding the Bargaining Session

It's always a good idea to establish an ending time in advance because it creates a logical, and neutral, separation point. For example, if, having received and discussed the other side's proposals, management says, "I think we're done for now" and leaves the table, it leaves a negative context that may not be intended. On the other hand, if four o'clock arrives, and the nominal ending time is four o'clock, the session simply ends with no negative context. If no ending time has been established, but additional time will be needed for counterproposals, it's reasonable to explain that a caucus would be too long, and it's more productive to end the session and begin when your side is able to respond. Regardless of timing, having received and reviewed each of the other side's proposals creates a logical stopping point. It also gives your team additional time to consider how it will respond to the just-received proposals. It's also a good idea to identify the issue or issues to be discussed at the next bargaining session so that both teams can focus their efforts in preparation for the next session.

The IBB Session

A lot has been accomplished before the initial IBB bargaining session: interests have been identified and exchanged, necessary data has been identified and shared, and all of the team members have undergone training and have individually made a commitment to the problem-solving process of IBB. Additionally, IBB is a managed process being overseen by a trained mediator whose role is to keep the parties in focus. So, with that in mind, let's start with a look at the bargaining table.

As you can see from the seating chart, the "us vs. them" context of the traditional bargaining session is removed, and each team member is seated adjacent to a member from the opposing bargaining team. Rather than each side sitting on one side of the table with the other side on the opposite side of the table, the IBB bargainers are asked to sit next to members of the opposite team, stressing the common interest of problem-solving. Likewise, the mediator and the individual team members, rather than the chief negotiators, will lead the discussions on a given issue.

The IBB bargaining interests of each side are both limited in number and presented in question format rather than in the form of proposed contract language. Each interest is presented as a problem to be collectively solved, with solutions recognizing the interests of both sides. The paper chase of formal written proposals and counterproposals is not a part of the IBB process at all. Because IBB is much less "scripted" than traditional bargaining, and each team member has a legitimate role to play, some amazing results—creative solutions never before considered—can come to the fore in IBB bargaining.

Ideas are always welcome in IBB bargaining discussions, but be careful of unintended consequences. Solutions that sound appealing at first glance can end up being entirely unworkable or unaffordable in practice. Remember that the goal of IBB bargaining is the "win-win" solution that serves the interests of both the union members and the enterprise. Be sure to articulate management's interests and evaluate each proposed solution in terms of how well it addresses management's interests. Solutions that fail to serve those interests should be rejected promptly.

TURNING SOLUTIONS INTO CONTRACT LANGUAGE

Once the IBB bargaining teams have, by consensus, identified an acceptable solution to an issue, it falls to the chief negotiators for each side to develop contract language that incorporates the agreed concepts into the contract. That language is then circulated among the bargaining teams and, if agreed upon, becomes a tentative agreement for the issues under discussion.[5] More about tentative agreements later.

IBB bargaining sessions are usually scheduled for a consecutive two- or three-day period. Since there are no formal written proposals and no formal written counterproposals, fewer issues, and an accelerated pace of discussions, many contracts are negotiated to conclusion in that time frame.

To this point I'm sure you would agree that IBB sounds attractive when compared with traditional bargaining. But generally there are no creative solutions to problems that cost money, and money issues lie at the heart of every collective bargaining exercise. Thus, when the discussions turn to wage, salary, and other money-driven issues, the parties tend to become positional, whether they mean to or not. In later chapters we'll address ways to overcome these problems. At this point, suffice that you understand that as attractive as it may sound, IBB is not an easy answer to fundamental financial issues.

As you review the other side's initial proposals you may find yourself wondering how agreement can ever be reached, given the magnitude of demands from the other side. But remember, you are at the beginning of the journey, not the end. Negotiations is the process of moving from extremes to workable solutions, and that process is now under way. In the next chapter we will talk about the next step: developing counterproposals and moving toward resolution of the issues.

CHAPTER 8

They Want...WHAT?

Responding to Union Demands

What follows is primarily, though not exclusively, focused on traditional bargaining, where formal written proposals are submitted with the expectation that the other side will respond in a similar fashion. Though written from the management perspective, the comments are equally relevant to union responses to management demands.

So, we've had our initial meeting, received the union's proposals, and now we are trying to figure out what to do next. Those new to the traditional bargaining process, especially on the management side, are usually shocked when they review the initial proposals of the labor side. The proposals appear outrageous, excessive, and impossible to agree to. But remember, it's bargaining, and as I have often advised clients, "It's their job to ask and your job to say no." So, put aside the sticker shock and focus on moving the process forward.

WORDS MATTER

Before we begin talking about counterproposals, I want to emphasize the importance of language. The drafting of language is one of the most important aspects of bargaining, and the management team needs to pay close attention to the wording of every proposal and counterproposal. Remember, it's a contract that you're negotiating, and as you review the union's proposals, keep in mind that what you're looking at is proposed language for that contract, but from the union's point of view. If the proposal is agreed to as presented, the language will be included exactly as written and will become an obligation of the enterprise.

Union negotiators are taught to draft proposals in broad language, placing all of the obligation on management, with little by way of qualification or exception. For example, suppose the teachers' union submits a proposal that goes something like, "the school district shall provide a qualified substitute teacher for each bargaining unit member absent from duty." The bargaining unit's motivation is to ensure some continuation of the lesson while the member is absent. Fine, but what about the possibility, often very real, that there simply is no qualified substitute teacher available for hire on that particular day? Other circumstances, far too numerous to mention here, could reasonably prevent management from complying with the language proposed for agreement, despite a lot of good-faith effort to do so. But, as presented, management's failure to comply, *for any reason*, constitutes a breach of the contract and could result in a grievance.

The point here is this: often the union simply doesn't care about management's compliance problems and has drafted its proposal to get the result that benefits its members. If management wants to impose conditions on its obligation it falls to management to do so by way of counterproposal. Thus, using our example, a management counter might look something like "the district will make a *reasonable effort* to provide qualified substitutes for bargaining unit members absent from the classroom due to *approved leaves of absence.*" Here, management's counter provides the essence of what the union wants, but with sufficient qualifications to prevent unintended violations of the contract when substitutes are not available. Likely, it would be agreed to by the union.

"Shall" is another favorite union term in bargaining proposals. Management "shall" provide… [some sort of benefit], with no obligation on the part of either the union or its members to do anything to initiate the action. Again, it falls to management to carefully consider the application and consequences of the union's proposal. If the concept is agreeable to management, develop a counter that makes it workable without the overly broad, one-sided application. If your chief negotiator is an experienced labor attorney, he or she can be of great help in this effort. Here's another example. The union proposes, "The governing board will grant paid sabbatical leave of one year to teachers who have completed five years of service." The governing board replies, "The governing board will consider and may grant sabbatical leave to teachers who have successfully completed at least five consecutive years of service, subject to the projected staffing needs of the district and the provisions of the Sabbatical leave policy." Here, the leave remains a possibility, but the board has vastly increased its ability to consider other relevant factors in making the decision.

As your team reviews the union's proposals, several questions should be kept in mind: (1) is there a genuine problem to be addressed, (2) how will the proposed change affect the operations of the enterprise, (3) what will it cost, (4) are there legitimate reasons to make any change and, (5) if changes are made, how can they be made in a way that is beneficial to the enterprise. Finally, are you sure that you have enough information to answer the foregoing questions?[1] Don't hesitate to bring in those managers who will be most directly affected by the union's proposals and get their assessment.

It is also important to remember that the development of counterproposals is not a one-time activity, at least with respect to many of the issues. The union's demand is responded to by management (or vice versa), the other side then responds to the counterproposal, and on and on until an agreement is reached. By far, the most difficult phase of the process is the development of the initial responses of management to the union's demand package. The point is, your first counterproposal may well not be your last with respect to many of the issues.

WHERE THE UNION'S PROPOSALS CAME FROM

Understanding the reasons behind the union's proposals is helpful when you are considering counterproposals. Earlier we noted some likely sources: issues not achieved in prior bargaining sessions and issues that have caused grievances during the existing contract. In addition, the statewide or national union organization often has specific contract goals for each of its locals and will encourage (i.e., require) that those goals be incorporated into the bargaining proposals of each local. One example of this was union proposals for "agency fee" dues deductions from non-union members of the bargaining unit, a provision no longer permitted.[2] Union proposals may also be based on the results of the local union's membership survey taken in anticipation of bargaining. Here, the members get to voice their wishes for contract changes to their wages and working conditions.[3] As you review the union's proposals, you will note that the realities of operation for the enterprise are often inconsistent with the wishes of individual union members. For example, a school bus driver begins his or her day at 6:30 a.m. in order to deliver the pupils to each of their respective schools before the beginning of the school day. The bus driver might prefer to sleep in and begin the day at 7:30 a.m., and the union proposes a change in the start of the day for bus drivers to 7:30 a.m. Although this may be convenient for the bus drivers, it would also entail changing the starting times for each of the schools, thus impacting each of the pupils, their family members, each of the teachers, and all of the support staff as well. Thus, what may seem like a very simple proposal may have far-reaching consequences that should be considered in developing management's responses. This is not to say that union proposals can't have value to the enterprise or that they should never be agreed to. I've seen some very intuitive, beneficial union proposals that management was happy to agree to.

FLAVORS OF "NO" – HARD OR SOFT

Remember that your legal obligation to engage in good-faith bargaining may require that you provide a response to each union proposal, but it does not include an obligation to agree with any proposal. You can, and in some cases should, just say "no." But, you are obliged to make a reasonable effort to find agreement where possible, and a "no" response to each and every union proposal is not, on its face, suggestive of that kind of effort. For example, suppose that our school bus drivers who wanted to sleep in actually had several other proposals as a part of their original package—proposals that included route changes that made the operation more efficient and less costly. You might be able to agree to that part of their package with a tweak or two, even though the remainder was unacceptable. So, you need to consider each aspect of the package and look for what can be agreed to as part of your response.

In bargaining there are two kinds of "no." One is "Hell no, not now, not ever" (the hard no); the other is more like "no, not today" (the soft no). There's a big difference in how the other side will read each of those "no" responses, and it's important that you craft your "no" with that distinction in mind. For example, if the proposal is one that you would not ever, under any circumstances agree to in any form, you shouldn't attempt to say "no" by making a counterproposal—even one that that you know the union can't agree to. Making *any* counter on an issue that you will not ever agree to is a mistake because it telegraphs the message that you "might" be willing to agree under the right circumstances. If your message is intended to be the "hard no," just say "no"—and make it clear that you mean it.

The soft "no" response, on the other hand, is often presented in such a way as to not preclude further discussion of the issue—if other changes in the union's position made that discussion potentially agreeable. Here's an example: Suppose the union wants to add a vacation day per year to the annual entitlement of each bargaining unit member. You might be able to do this, but it has a cost and, when viewed in conjunction with the other financial demands, the cost is simply too large. On the other hand, if that were the only cost item in the package and agreement guaranteed a settlement, you'd be willing to agree to the additional vacation day. In this example management might be willing to add the additional day, but only if it was part of an entire package that met spending expectations. So, it could counter with a proposal to defer further discussion of that issue until the discussion of financial issues, because it is (at least to management), a financial issue. Another possibility would be to offer a counter that gave an additional vacation day—but only to unit members with thirty or more years of service. Either one of those options would be far less than agreement with the proposal as presented, but not a "Hell no." There are numerous other possible responses, limited only by the creativity of the management bargaining team.

Another common initial management response to union proposals is "CCL," short for "current contract language" which, in effect, says that management is offering no change to the current language affected by the proposal. It is a form of counter-proposal that simply says, "no change." And while management bargaining team members might want to make that the response to *every* union proposal, keep in mind the "good faith" obligation. You need to be able to demonstrate a good-faith effort to reach agreement, and some proposals may merit more than simply saying "no" or "CCL."

Another potential response to a union's proposal may be to turn it around and make it work in management's favor. This is done by a counterproposal that flips the obligations imposed on management by the union's proposal to the union, making the benefits conditional or optional and requiring the union members to take the initiative. Here's an extreme example, offered solely to make the point. Suppose the union proposal would require each day of employee absence to be automatically treated as paid leave, regardless of whether the employee was sick or otherwise legitimately absent from work. Extreme, yes, but not beyond the realm of possibility. Rather than "Hell no," management might choose to reply with a counterproposal that would impose a requirement for advance notice by the employee of any intended absence (including sick leave), deduction of two days of earned sick leave credit for each day of absence leave used, and the use of absence leave only by employees who have accrued a minimum of sixty days of sick leave. This is an example of the kind of counterproposal that you know will likely not be acceptable to the union. At the same time, the concept of "personal leave" as reflected in the union's proposal is not entirely foreign to many public sector contracts, especially teaching contracts, and if pursued further by the union there may be acceptable compromises that could be agreed to even though management's initial counterproposal likely will not be acceptable. But whether accepted or not, it is a reply to the union's proposal and should satisfy the good-faith bargaining standard. The union, at that point, could simply withdraw the proposal and move on.

Management's counterproposals will hopefully result in some of the union's initial proposals being withdrawn, but in other cases the union may reply with a modified version of its demand that is closer to being acceptable to management. This may signal that the issue is of importance to the union and warrants a closer look to see if compromises can be made that might satisfy the issue. Remember, the goal is not to simply say "no," but to find ways to reach ultimate agreement.

TIMING

Collective bargaining is more art than science and one of the most artful choices to be made is the timing of concessions in bargaining. Understand that the exact same proposal could: (1) result in a successful resolution of the issue under discussion, (2) result in the successful conclusion of the entire negotiations or, (3) move the parties farther apart if made at the wrong time.

Unfortunately, there's no clock to guide the timing of bargaining proposals because every negotiation is unique and mainly, but not exclusively, governed by four factors: (1) the bargaining history of the parties, (2) the nature of the issues being discussed, (3) the personalities of the bargaining team members on each side and, (4) where you are in your current negotiations. The best judge of these factors is usually the person on the bargaining team with the most experience, and this is yet another example of why you should have a chief negotiator who is experienced in dealing with the union's organization and, hopefully, the union's chief negotiator in a variety of other negotiations. Suffice to say at this point that every management response should be considered not only based on good faith and workability, but also on the timing of the process.

MOTIVATION

Collective bargaining is as much an exercise in psychology as it is of economics. Consideration of the personalities of the union's bargaining team can be a major factor in the analysis of the union's proposals. Here, keep in mind that the motivations of all of the individuals on the team may well not be the same. For the union's bargaining representative (chief negotiator) bargaining is a job, and agreement at your enterprise means little more than moving on to another bargaining round somewhere else. The employee members of the team are often far differently motivated, and for many of them, bargaining can evoke strong personal emotions and fears. For example, once, deep into discussions of major changes to the employee health plan, the union president confided that she had been told by her membership that they really didn't care what she did in bargaining but, "don't mess with the health plan." For her, the discussions evoked images of her standing in front of her membership and announcing that the team had done exactly that which she had been expressly told not to do. Understanding that fear can be a great help in crafting counters that have some chance of success. In that instance, we managed to overcome her fear by having the mediator agree to present the health plan revisions to the union and by providing extensive, one-on-one training for the union members on each of the aspects of the new plan.

Another form of motivation is the personal bias of bargaining unit members. While in theory all union proposals represent the collective benefit of the unit members, that's not quite how it works out in practice. For example, I once bargained with a teachers' union team whose member had a transsexual child whom he believed had been harassed and discriminated against in high school, and he was set on getting provisions into the negotiated agreement prohibiting such discrimination. He saw bargaining as a forum to advance his own agenda and was set on doing so.[4] We'll have more to say about motivation later.

Management team members are no less subject to the tendency to insert personal agendas into the bargaining process, and that tendency should be resisted as much as possible. The soundest approach is to consider what's in the best interest of the enterprise and focus on achieving that end.

BARGAINING BASICS

Just as the union really didn't expect you to agree to all of their proposals out of hand, you shouldn't expect to present one round of counterproposal and have it agreed to. Traditional negotiation is a process, and part of that process is for each side to determine that it has gotten as much as it can on each issue. As you consider your counterproposals, plan for the possibility that you won't achieve agreement and may have to move "just a little" further to get agreement. For example, they want ten (somethings), and you're willing to give four to get agreement. Don't counter with four the first time around; offer one and leave yourself room to move later. The number of additional counters to plan for will depend on the nature of the issue, the amount of progress being made and the number of remaining issues yet to be resolved.

Here are a couple of additional basics to keep in mind. First, if you are a card player you have likely heard the adage, "a card laid is a card played" meaning that once a card is on the table it can't be withdrawn and a different card played. Much the same is true in collective bargaining. Going backward without a good reason is considered evidence of bad faith and is not an appropriate strategy.

Here's an example: Suppose two people are negotiating the sale of a horse. Seller asks $10; buyer offers $2. In the next round, the seller comes down to $7 and buyer offers $5. You would expect a deal to be made at $6, but the seller, surprisingly, changes his offer, going backward to $8. This is an over-simplified example of backward or "regressive" bargaining, which is generally unacceptable in collective bargaining. This is not to say that offers can't be changed when there is good reason to do so, even if the change reduces the value of one or more components included in a previous offer.

Here's another example: Suppose the union wants a $1 per hour pay raise and additional insurance benefits costing the equivalent of an additional $.20 per hour. Management has offered the $1 raise—but with no additional insurance benefits. In the next round management offers the $.20 insurance benefit—but reduces the pay raise offer to $.80. The combined monetary value of the second offer is identical to the first, but the numbers are in different places. In my view, that's a perfectly reasonable offer and not regressive bargaining. But it's important to be aware of the potential issue as your draft counters.

Another basic tenet of bargaining is to never counter your own proposal. In traditional bargaining, every proposal merits a response, even if the response is "no" or "CCL." Until you get a response from the other side to a proposal, don't offer a counter.

KEEPING SCORE

Keeping track of what was done, and when, is a complex process, especially in traditional bargaining where there may be numerous proposals and counterproposals before reaching agreement on any issue. It is a good idea early on to develop an index of the issues proposed on each side so you can track when each of the union's issues was responded to and the status of that issue as negotiations move forward. Knowing the status of each issue can be of tremendous help if disputes arise in the future. The best time to begin the record-keeping process is during the development of initial counterproposals.

Your bargaining team is now familiar with all of the proposals and has developed counterproposals to many of the union's initial demands. It's now time to begin the work of negotiating acceptable compromises and drafting them as contract language as the bargaining teams move from initial proposals to agreement on specific issues and, finally, agreement on a final contract. In the next chapter we will talk about how all of that happens.

CHAPTER 9

Moving to
Agreement

We have now moved from our initial traditional
bargaining meeting to the development of our first
round of counterproposals, and we are now ready to meet with
the union's bargaining team once again. From this point to the
beginning of economic discussions, the sequence of activity
should look something like: (1) bargaining meeting for discussion of specific agenda item and review of proposals and counterproposals related to that item, (2) caucus by each team, (3)
resumption of bargaining meeting with tentative agreement on
one or more of the issues under discussion, and then on to the
next issue.

At the outset, the collective proposals from each side add up
to a substantial number of complex issues with little if any room
for agreement. You may well be asking, "How can we possibly
proceed from this point to the ultimate goal of a final contract?"
By way of contrast, if we were bargaining in the IBB model we
would have far fewer issues to deal with and a mediator to manage
the discussions. But that's a different chapter.[1]

SEQUENCING ISSUE DISCUSSIONS

Generally, the bargaining teams, through their chief negotiators, will decide where to begin. In many cases, the parties simply move through the existing contract from front to back and address each issue for which a proposed change has been offered, setting aside the direct-dollar cost items to the end. If there is an issue about which both sides have proposed changes, all of the proposed changes should be addressed at the same time. Likewise, if there are two related issues, even though appearing in different parts of the contract, they should also be addressed at the same time.

For example, the contract has provisions for long-term leaves of various types. Perhaps the leave provisions include disability leave, sabbatical leave, long-term sick leave, etc. Those provisions each address the status of substitutes hired to take the place of the absent bargaining unit member on leave. One or both sides want to change that status as relates to one of the leave provisions. However, management is concerned that administration of the contract becomes more difficult with different provisions for each type of leave, especially when there is no substantive reason for different provisions. Thus, it's better to address all of them at once, both for a clearer understanding of the contract and for its effective administration. Simpler is better.

In my experience, the most successful agenda is one that sequences issues from the least to the most difficult, recognizing that the two sides may disagree about the level of difficulty to be ascribed to any particular proposal. The least difficult are usually the "cleanup" editorial issues in the current contract, while the most difficult are the substantive issues of salary, benefits, and other economic issues. Experienced negotiators have a good sense of what issues are more difficult than others and what proposals have the seeds of agreement lying within. It's always a positive sign if the chief negotiators on each side can agree on a sequence of issues, and though often unstated, the easier issues are addressed in the earlier parts of the negotiations and the more difficult issues toward the latter part.

As we noted earlier, salary and economic benefit items are nearly always discussed last. Management generally prefers to defer the discussion of those issues until the end of the bargaining rather than earlier in order to save its strongest leverage for last.

Additionally, keep in mind that many bargaining issues brought for discussion by the union will also entail additional cost. Management needs to be able to judge the entire cost of the contract as well as the cost of each item. Recognizing that salary and benefits will be the largest, but not the only cost items in the contract, it's wise to determine the cost of each item under discussion so it can, if agreed to, be added to the total cost when the salary and benefit issues are reached. Issues that represent substantial additional cost should also be moved to the back of the queue and discussed in conjunction with economic issues.

WATCH THE LANGUAGE

I seldom accept any proposal exactly as drafted by the union. Even if the concept is agreeable, every word matters. Clarity is important, and even more important is filling in the parts left out of the union proposal. Back to our substitute teacher example, the commitment to provide a substitute for an absent unit member is always conditioned on the availability of the substitute. So, with those thoughts in mind, let the bargaining team decide what changes are agreeable, and let the chief negotiator draft and present the counters. Make sure you can live with any proposal or counterproposal before saying "yes," but when the terms are agreeable, don't hesitate to say "yes."

THE SEARCH FOR TENTATIVE AGREEMENT

The whole point of bargaining is to reach agreement on all of the outstanding negotiations issues. That generally happens in small increments rather than all at one time. Issue agreement, as opposed to agreement on the entire contract, is generally referred to as "tentative agreement." The issue agreements are "tentative" because they only become final when all of the bargaining issues have been agreed to and the entire package has been ratified by the governing bodies of both the union and the enterprise. Issue agreement can take one of three forms: (1) agreement to withdraw a proposal, leaving existing contract language in place, (2) agreement to amend existing language with the new language having been agreed to by both sides, or (3) agreement to an entirely new contract provision. In any of these events, the issue agreement is reduced to writing, initialed (or signed) by the chief negotiators for each side to indicate that tentative agreement has been reached on that issue. Once tentative agreement has been reached, the bargaining of the issues included in the tentative agreement is also finished, and the parties move on to the next issue on the agenda. Any later attempt to change what has been agreed to in a tentative agreement will most certainly be rejected by the other side.

Defining the Problem

At this stage of bargaining, the discussions should be focused on efforts to identify the specific problem the proposal under discussion is attempting to fix. Good questions can lead to valuable information, and it's important for each team member to listen carefully to what is said. Solving the problem may well require a different proposal from the one currently on the table. As noted earlier, a traditional bargaining rule says that a team should never, ever, counter its own proposal. If the discussions lead to a solution, and management made the last proposal, it falls to the union to propose the solution, not management.

Comparative data is important and far more available now than in the past. If, for example, the union has asked for a specific type of leave in addition to those already available, for instance, "deceased pet leave" and management is able to point out, accurately, that no other public employer in the county has any similar type of leave and, further, that the leave provisions already available to the bargaining unit are far more generous than most of the other public employee contracts, the union's position becomes very difficult to maintain. It is helpful for each side to develop comparative data that relates to its bargaining demands and often essential in the case of salary and benefit demands.

In many cases there are no easy solutions, and it appears that a fundamental disagreement exists between the two bargaining teams. Nonetheless, it is important to determine *exactly* what it is that the two sides disagree about because, unless resolved, the issue will prevent the parties from reaching final agreement. It is important to identify these issues as early as possible. Once a "blocking issue" is identified, and the nature of the problem understood, put it aside and move on through the remainder of the bargaining issues.[2]

Your planning meetings should have identified a range of possible counterproposals to deal with specific union issues. As the discussions evolve, it may be appropriate to make additional counters within that range in an effort to move the discussion forward. As a matter of personal strategy, however, I have made it a practice to never exhaust my authority (i.e. offer the most my team was authorized to offer) unless I was certain that by doing so we would reach tentative agreement on that issue. How did I know that it would make the deal? See the "watercooler" discussion that soon follows.

At this point you may well be wondering how all of this actually works. For illustration only, let's go back to the union's proposal for paid leave for deceased pets and follow a possible sequence of discussions:

- Union proposes—up to fifteen days per year paid leave for deceased pet.
- Management responds—no (soft no).
- Union counters—up to five days per year, same conditions.
- Management counters—one day deceased pet leave in any five-year period.
- Union counters—three days per year.
- Management counters—add "deceased pet leave" to reasons for using existing personal leave.
- Tentative agreement!

The above sequence shows how each side makes some movement toward the other side's position as discussions move forward. At the end, management gave the union what it wanted, but without expanding any existing paid leave provisions and the union got what it wanted, the opportunity to use paid leave to mourn for Buffy.

PACKAGE BARGAINING

Moving to ultimate agreement is an incremental process of finding the points of agreement between what management is willing to give and what labor is willing to accept and vice versa. Sometimes that agreement happens with respect to single issues, and in other cases, it involves looking at multiple issues at the same time. In many cases, usually after the very beginning stages of bargaining but before the final stages, the teams will move into "package bargaining" mode. Package bargaining involves structuring several issues into a single counterproposal in hopes of eliminating some of them and finding agreement on others.

For example, the offer might go something like, "The board will agree to the following counterproposal on issue 'a' if the union will agree to current language on issues 'c,' 'd,' and 'e' and agree to withdraw issue 'f.'" In the package, five issues are addressed, but only one of them offers a contract change. However, if agreed, five issues are resolved. The counter on issue "a" makes a concession to the union's initial demand, but in a context that works for management. Often the package will be met with a counterproposal from the union, also in the form of a package, but if it moves bargaining forward and resolves one or more issues, it may well be agreeable to management. Be aware that a union package counterproposal may not necessarily contain the same issues as those in management's package. Each package should be thoroughly evaluated on its own, regardless of the initial proposal that it purports to respond to.

While packages are great ways to get through negotiations with large numbers of issues, the benefit can be lost if you use that technique too early or try to include too many "high-value" (to the union) issues in the package. Once package bargaining is commenced, it tends to become the norm for the remainder of the negotiations. But management can't begin package bargaining too early because it's viewed by the union side as an unwillingness to consider the union's individual proposals. After those proposals have been reviewed, discussed, and rejected, a package that gives the union something (as opposed to nothing) will begin to look better.

It's always best to begin package bargaining with a small package limited to two or three issues and increase the number of issues in later packages. Packages tend to be more successful if they contain proposals (both union and management) that relate to the same general topic, such as leaves, working conditions, etc. One of the benefits of a package proposal is that it gives a clearer picture of the relative value the union has assigned to its proposals. Low-value issues may be dropped, but the higher-value issues will continue to be in dispute. Both the timing and structure of package bargaining proposals involve judgments based on the unique circumstances of your bargaining at the time.

SIDEBAR – THE WATER COOLER IS YOUR FRIEND

Especially in traditional bargaining, statements made at the bargaining table are presumed to reflect the position of the side whose negotiator is making the statement. There is virtually no chance for informal sidebar "off-the-record" discussions. At the same time, there is a great deal of information that might help move negotiations forward—if only some candid sidebar discussions with the leadership of the other side could take place.

Sidebar discussions usually don't begin until the mid-point of negotiations or later. As a practical matter, the discussions usually take place during a caucus and usually involve only the chief negotiator for each side and the highest-ranking other individual for each side. The meeting usually takes place, for example, in the hall at the water cooler or outside at the flagpole—any nearby location out of the presence of the other team members or onlookers. The purpose of the sidebar is to try to find options that would be acceptable to the other side when agreement can't be reached on the issue or issues under discussion. If a mediator is engaged in the negotiations at that point, whether because it's an IBB bargaining or because the parties have requested mediation, the mediator should also be included in the discussions.

Sidebar discussions are "off the record" and tend to focus on issues that were discussed in the previous bargaining session. Clarification is important, and questions like, "Do we correctly understand that your position on _____ is _____?" But, if you are getting close to a final agreement, it is fair game to explore what the other side's reaction might be to a "what-if" proposal under consideration by your side.

Trust can become a major asset in sidebar discussions. If the chief negotiators trust each other to do what they say they will do, sidebars can be tremendously helpful. If that trust is lacking, they are worthless or even counterproductive. As negotiations move along, the issues tend to become more difficult and the need for sidebar discussions more intense. But keep in mind that the union's lead negotiator works for his or her team, and if the team believes that the serious negotiations are taking place over the watercooler, with them out of the action, they may become unhappy with their negotiator. Thus, seasoned union negotiators will tend to use sidebar discussions sparingly. Nearly every final agreement is preceded by a sidebar conversation.

WORKING THROUGH DISAGREEMENT

It is not uncommon for the discussions at the bargaining table to reveal that the parties are far apart on a given issue. This circumstance calls for strategic evaluation on the part of your bargaining team. First, you should consider where you are in the bargaining process. If you are in the early stages of bargaining with lots of potentially problematic issues yet to be dealt with, it may be best to put this one aside and move on. On the other hand, if this is the only remaining issue to achieving a final deal you have every incentive to continue working toward agreement on the issue. As we have said before, timing is everything.

Working through difficult issues generally involves a willingness to compromise, either on the issue under discussion or on some other issue important to the other side. Compromise is a two-way street, and if the other side is unwilling to compromise, movement on your part will secure no progress. Compromise can take many forms; here's one example showing a range of different positions management might take. The contract provides for three days of personal leave for teachers in the bargaining unit. Use of those days is conditioned upon one of a long list of circumstances (limitations) that must be present. The list includes circumstances personal to the teacher, such as court appearances, graduation of a child, buying a house, etc. The teachers want to remove the list, thus making the use of personal days "unlimited." The governing board is concerned that removal of the list will cause a sharp increase in the use of personal leave and increase its labor cost by requiring the hiring of more substitutes. In addition, the absence of the regular teacher from the classroom can have a negative impact on the pupils' learning opportunities.

In its team caucus, the board's bargaining team (with the approval of the governing board as well) has determined that this is a "soft no" issue for the board.[3] While it doesn't want to remove the restrictions, it would possibly be willing to do so in lieu of a strike. So, how does the management team counter that proposal? Here are a few suggestions: (1) no, but not a "Hell No," (2) counter with some of the restrictions removed and tighter requirements for advance notice of the leave request and availability of a qualified substitute, (3) counter with a proposed deferral of the discussion to the salary and benefits portion of the negotiations, (4) "package" the board's counter, assuming some concessions are made, with other issues under discussion.

The foregoing is not a suggested solution but an example of the process of working through competing interests at the bargaining table. Many union proposals are simply rejected by management with no compromise offered, and we are not suggesting that there is an obligation to seek compromise on any union proposal. But keep in mind that management rejection of *all* union proposals, without a demonstrable effort to compromise, will have a difficult time passing the good-faith bargaining requirement.

THE IBB BARGAINING MEETING

The IBB bargaining meeting offers a stark contrast to the confrontational style of traditional bargaining. Note some of the differences:

- The parties are not seated on opposite sides of the table; union team members are seated next to management team members.
- Discussions are led by the mediator, not by a spokesperson for either side with the interests of each side presented by a team member.
- There are no written proposals or counterproposals; each side presents its bargaining issues in the form of "interests."
- Each side has limited the number of issues that it brings to the table, usually to ten or so, excluding salary and benefits.

The IBB mediator directs the discussions at the meeting. Either the mediator or a designated bargaining team member will keep a running record of the discussions on a flip chart or computer screen projected on the wall for all to see. The issue under discussion is noted, and the interests of each bargaining team in that issue will also be noted. Possible solutions will be advanced and discussed by members of each bargaining team. Potential solutions will be evaluated based on whether they serve the interests of both the labor and management teams. When a mutually agreed solution has been reached, the contract language will be drafted by either the chief negotiators or other designated individuals while the bargaining teams move on to the next issue.

Caucus meetings are available in IBB bargaining and are often used. However, unlike with a traditional bargaining caucus, the mediator may ask the team calling the caucus to describe the gist of what was discussed in its meeting for the entire group.

This is not to suggest that all issues are resolved in IBB bargaining; they are not. But the benefits of collaborative problem-solving often produce far better and faster results than traditional bargaining.

The initial IBB meeting is often scheduled to last a day, and in many instances, the entire bargaining process is completed or nearly completed within that time. Even if not fully resolved, the vast majority of issues have been resolved, and what remains are points of fundamental disagreement, "blocking issues." Regardless of the bargaining process followed, blocking issues need to be addressed and resolved, and the next chapter will describe how that process works.

CHAPTER 10

Money Talk

In previous chapters we talked about deferring the discussion of salary and benefit proposals to the later part of bargaining. Now, having addressed the other issues and, hopefully, having resolved most if not all of them, it's time to have "the money" talk. Perhaps the single most important aspect of financial discussions is to try to have everyone working from the same basic facts regarding the enterprise's finances. In most, if not all, states, the financial data regarding units of local government is public data. There is nothing to hide, nor should there be. Thus, the relevant data should be presented clearly and accurately, before the negotiation of monetary issues begins. The presentation should include the data relative to the ability of the enterprise to approve pay or benefit increases, such as the cost of the current salary and benefit package, projected year-end carryover balances or deficits, projected increases or decreases in operating revenue, and other factors related to the ability of the enterprise to pay salary and benefits. Usually these data are compiled and presented by the enterprise's chief fiscal officer. It may also be relevant to know where the enterprise stands with respect to the area labor market.

Are current pay and benefits at or near the market for similar jobs in similar enterprises?

The second most important aspect of bargaining wages and benefits is the ability to cost proposals quickly and accurately. In the planning stages, we talked about the development of wage-cost spreadsheets that would enable management to cost a proposal or counterproposal quickly and accurately. Now is the time to roll those spreadsheets out and be ready to use them. Things can move very quickly toward the end of bargaining, and extended delays while proposals are costed can be harmful to the process.

In IBB bargaining, the financial presentation usually takes place as part of the preparation for bargaining, and the data has already been compiled and shared before the actual bargaining session begins. In traditional bargaining, it is certainly possible to have the financial discussion before the bargaining begins, but often it takes place during the actual bargaining sessions. Here the usual protocol is put aside for the fiscal presentation, and the chief fiscal officer takes the floor. Keep in mind that salary and benefits are emotional issues for some union bargaining team members, and the ability of the enterprise to give pay raises is far less important than the perceived needs of the members to receive those raises. However, sound bargaining should be based on facts, not emotion.

Regardless of bargaining style, the goal at this point in your negotiations is to offer a package proposal, the acceptance of which will resolve all outstanding issues and conclude negotiations. Often the incentive of a monetary offer will help unblock some of the issues that were in disagreement before. If either side has additional concessions to make on those issues, now is the time to consider making them.

MOTIVATION

One of the greatest challenges—and greatest sources of satisfaction—in collective bargaining lies in finding just the right combination that will satisfy both sides and bring negotiations to a successful conclusion. In difficult bargaining situations, that combination usually involves the right proposal made at the right time. It has been my experience that negotiations settle when they are ready, and not before. Knowing when it's time is more art than science, but it helps to consider some of the motivating factors in play.

First, on the union side, the membership wants bargaining to happen, but they also want it over with. For them, bargaining means uncertainty. Will I get a raise? Will my healthcare benefits change? Will I be asked to go on strike? All of these and more contribute to the uncertainty that bargaining brings for the membership. The passage of time only adds to that uncertainty.

Likewise, bargaining creates uncertainty for management as well. In the school setting, for example, the ongoing issues of whether there will be a teachers' (or non-teaching employee) strike and how busy families deal with the logistics of all of that can permeate discussions for school families. Those concerns flow through to the governing board, and the management employees as well. On the management side, some of the other issues also carry grave concerns. For example, if management believes that giving the financial benefit package demanded by the union will bankrupt the school district in short order, the threat of a school strike puts them between a "rock and hard place" because there is no acceptable alternative available.

The ever-present third party in public sector negotiations is the taxpaying public that receives the bargained-for services. Public perception of collective bargaining can have an enormous impact on the outcome. One example is an ill-advised teacher strike that was called by the union some years ago. After about ten days it became clear that parents, and the public in general, simply had no support for the strike, and they strongly pressured the bargaining unit members, who were also their neighbors and friends, to give it up. Needless to say, the strike totally collapsed, and the union was forced to accept management's last offer. Even though the public's attitude toward the potential for a strike is important, it's rare that it will have such a profound impact. Nonetheless, it's always a factor.

One of the goals of both sides should be to avoid the collective uncertainty that accompanies labor unrest and to avoid a strike. As we said earlier, timing is one of the keys. For both negotiating teams, a final settlement cannot take place until the team members believe they have fully satisfied their obligations by bargaining as fully and effectively as they can, and getting the best deal for their respective members that they can. Sometimes that can take place in a day; often, it takes longer.

BRIDGING THE INFORMATION GAP

Disagreement can come about for a number of reasons. The union, for example, can believe that management's proposal offers them no benefit or that it would be unacceptable to the rank-and-file membership. Management, on the other hand, may believe that the union's proposal would be too difficult to administer or would cost too much. These are fundamental disagreements that the parties will have to overcome, if possible, in negotiations.

A more substantive disagreement often arises as negotiations approach the final stage and the teams are talking seriously about wages and benefits. Initially, the union's wage and benefit proposals often pay little heed to affordability. After all, it's their job to ask. But as negotiations proceed, cost and affordability become significant issues for both sides, and sharing a common factual ground for decision-making becomes critical. For example, suppose the union has asked for a 10% pay increase for the coming year. The union's finance committee has reviewed the enterprise's fiscal budget and agrees that the figures contained in that budget don't support a 10% increase. But, the union argues, the enterprise has always budgeted a shortfall and, somehow, always ends the fiscal year in the black. So, why not agree to the raise?

Public finance is a difficult challenge for many branches of local government. Even the best data, analyzed in good faith, can end up far off the mark, either on the plus or minus side. For management, the safest approach is to not spend money it clearly doesn't have and not to gamble on tax increases to bail them out if they spend themselves into a hole. Bridging the gap between the union's view that its members merit a substantial raise and management's view that it can't afford that raise is key to finding resolution. There's no easy answer, but credibility is the most important part of that bridge. If the fiscal officer lacks credibility with the union, the analysis will be challenged. Some unions will bring in their own fiscal analysis and present the management's negotiations team with a scenario that fully supports their raise proposal. When faced with different analyses of issues that important, it's incumbent on both the union and management to fully understand where and why the differences arise. The issue is not whose financial analysis is more reliable, it's about the facts that make up the financial picture. Determine the facts and make sure that both sides understand those facts. Without agreement on fiscal reality, moving forward in negotiations is difficult. How? Well, in some cases, third parties with credibility on both sides of the table can be brought in. In other circumstances, a union subcommittee meets with the fiscal officer and chief negotiator to review in depth every aspect of the analysis.

The acknowledgment of basic finances impacting negotiations doesn't necessarily mean agreement on the size of the salary and benefit package, but it is a good start. From there, the next step may be agreement on a process to be followed in determining the salary and benefit issues.

There will be some members of the union's team for whom the facts are irrelevant because they simply "want a raise," and that belief of entitlement overwhelms considerations of affordability. But for others, the realities of affordability will help them move toward agreement, even though the result is far from what they had hoped for. The overarching reality in the public sector is that the enterprise is unable to engage in deficit spending, and if the enterprise commits to a pay scale that it can't afford it will be forced to reduce staff to avoid a shortfall. Jobs will be lost, services to the public will suffer, and everyone loses. But, getting to agreement in that scenario first requires a common understanding of the essential facts.

Looking for Compromise

Creative structuring of proposals can sometimes make all the difference. At this point in your bargaining, you are exchanging packages of proposals that, if agreed to, would conclude negotiations, but the parties are unable to agree because one or more parts of the package is unacceptable. Here are six examples of ways to modify proposals in such a way as to potentially make the entire package acceptable.

Signing Bonus

Assume that you are very close to agreement on a new three-year contract. All of the outstanding issues except the size of the pay raise have been agreed upon. The teachers want a 3% raise for each year of the contract, and management believes that it can afford an increase, but something smaller than 3%. Consider offering a "signing bonus" payment that will be paid to each bargaining unit member within xxx days after the contract is approved. The bonus is a monetary cost but not subject to annual increases because it is not included in the contracted salary schedule, thus, reducing the overall cost of the package to management.

Back-load the Salary Schedule

Another way to package pay increases is to load the higher percentage increases into the later years of the contract. Percentage increases are cumulative from year to year; a 3% increase in the first year of the contract will be paid in each of the subsequent years of the contract. Thus, if you cost out two salary packages, one with 3% the first year, 2% the second year, and 1% the third year against a package that reverses the order of increase to pay 1% in year one, 2% in year two and 3% in year three, you will find that the latter is less costly.

CONTINGENT PAY RAISES

Sometimes agreements can be reached by making pay increases in later years of the contract contingent on the availability of funds to pay the increases. For example, the union wants a 3% pay raise in the third year of the contract. Management would be willing to give the raise if it knew that the funding to pay for it would be present. Current funding uncertainties make it impossible to predict the availability of that funding. To overcome this problem, management proposes to grant the increase, but *only* if its carryover funding balance as of a date certain in the future equals or exceeds a specified amount. The amount specified would be sufficient to fund the proposed pay raise.

Contingent proposals can be a useful tool in the bargaining toolbox, but be careful how you use them. Unions generally dislike contingent benefits due to the uncertainty. Management may also have reason to dislike contingent benefits because of the commitment of future resources. For example, a salary increase conditioned on the passage of a tax levy essentially puts the raise up for vote by the community. Communities generally tend to reject levies tied to employee raises.

SHORTEN THE LENGTH
OF THE CONTRACT

Time is always a variable in bargaining, and it can sometimes be used to reach the magical "yes" moment. If, for example, the parties have bargained on both sides for a three-year contract and simply cannot reach agreement on a salary package for three years, another option is to offer a two-year contract. Granted, both sides want three years, but a certain two-year agreement sometimes looks far more appealing than continuing to try to negotiate a three-year deal that is out of reach. A similar approach would have the parties agree on a three-year contract but gives the union the right to reopen negotiations on a limited number of issues, such as salary and benefits, for the final year of the contract.

CREATE A STUDY COMMITTEE

Committees are not good solutions for salary and benefit issues, where the only variables are cost and funding. But many proposals, even pay-related proposals, can involve the development of information and proposed solutions that could involve a great deal of time and effort to fully understand. Sometimes these issues can be resolved by referring it to a study committee made up of both labor and management members. The committee is charged with the duty to study the issue and make recommendations. Here's an example: Assume that a school district has a large list of "supplemental contracts," additional duties, and pay for such things as football coach, yearbook advisor, debate team advisor, etc. Further assume that the union has asked for an across-the-board increase of 10% for each of those positions. Management believes that some positions are already overpaid and refuses to give an across-the-board increase but would consider increasing pay for some of the positions if there were data showing the need for the increase. In this example, the study committee would be charged with reviewing each of the positions and making a payroll recommendation for each of them. With this agreement, the contract is approved and ratified by both the union and governing board, but without any changes to the supplemental pay schedule other than the agreement to create the study committee and review its recommendations.

The recommendations of the study committee will be made to the bargaining teams, and a mutually agreed change to the collective bargaining agreement necessary to implement those recommendations. To accomplish this, both the union and governing board will be required to agree to the changes to the contract. At that point neither side is committed to approving the changes, but good faith requires due consideration of the committee's recommendations.

Both sides tacitly understand that committees are handy ways to get disputed issues "off the table" without having to make a decision at the bargaining table. In practice, however, the committees are often simply never implemented, and the same issue returns at the next bargaining session still unresolved. This problem can be avoided by including strict timelines for the committee to commence and complete its work and report its results. If you're going to create a study committee, use it.

FOLD ADDITIONAL BENEFITS INTO EXISTING CONTRACT PROVISIONS

If one of your blocking issues is a proposal to create a new leave entitlement for the bargaining unit, consider the following as an alternative. Most contractual benefits, particularly leave provisions, have been around for a while, and the existence, use, and cost of those provisions have been established over time. Rather than creating new and untested leave entitlements, consider folding some additional entitlement into the existing structure. Doing so can offer the benefit of giving the union what it wants, but with limited cost to management.

Let's return to our previous example of a union proposal for paid leave for the loss of a pet. Suppose the union has proposed something like, "Bargaining unit members shall be granted paid bereavement leave for the loss of a treasured pet." To illustrate the range of options that might be considered, the first answer from management is a soft "no" with an explanation of the reasons. However, if it continues to be a blocking issue and management is willing to make some concession, the task becomes one of making the proposal acceptable to both sides. If, for example, the contract provides for personal leave that is limited to specified circumstances, you might consider adding "emotional distress from the loss of a household pet" as one of the circumstances that would permit the use of one of those days. Since the personal leave days are already part of the contract, the likely increased cost to management is small, and its addition might increase the chances of reaching an agreement.

The potential for creative solutions to blocking issues is vast, but not unlimited. In some instances the union wants exactly what it asked for—and nothing else. If what is asked for is unacceptable to management, there is a problem, and creativity is not the answer. Something needs to change, and you need to consider the next level of alternatives for the resolution of the outstanding issues, as discussed in the next chapter. If you are fortunate enough to have reached tentative agreement on a new contract you can exchange high-fives and proceed to Chapter 14, Agreement and Beyond.

CHAPTER 11

Dispute Resolution Strategies

At this point we assume that your bargaining meetings have reviewed every issue raised for bargaining and that you have reached tentative agreement on many of those issues. However, difficult issues remain unresolved, and additional progress appears unlikely because each side has become "dug in" on its position regarding those issues. What happens next? In this chapter we review the more common strategies for the resolution of disputes such as those just described. Two factors should be considered at the outset. First, dispute resolution is often dictated by state bargaining law or by the terms of an existing labor contract. We will describe some of the more common procedures, but it is important to know what the legal requirements are in your state. Second, all negotiations end—sometime.

IMPASSE

Impasse is a term of art in collective bargaining.[1] In layman's terms it means that all of the issues have been discussed, each side has made all of the compromises it's willing to make, and ultimate agreement is not possible (at this time). Some unions and governing boards have a history of always going to impasse before ultimate settlement, and for them it's an anticipated part of the process. In other cases, impasse is a new phase of bargaining. In either event, having attained a genuine condition of impasse is a critical phase of negotiations. First, it assumes that both sides have bargained in good faith and are unable to agree. Each has fulfilled its legal responsibility to the bargaining process thus far. Second, it means that each side is unwilling (at this time) to make any further concessions to reach agreement. Impasse results from a joint declaration of the negotiating teams stating that impasse has been reached in their negotiations.[2]

The options available to the parties at impasse are determined either by the terms of the current collective bargaining agreement, or by the law governing public sector collective bargaining in that jurisdiction. As mentioned earlier, special provisions often govern impasse in safety forces bargaining. But let's assume we are dealing with a bargaining unit of school bus drivers or some similar, non-safety forces group. The most common and, in my opinion, most effective procedure to overcome impasse is mediation. Note that it is generally not necessary to declare impasse to begin mediation, and in some states the parties must have mediated their dispute before they are permitted to declare impasse.[3]

MEDIATION

Mediation is a process in which a neutral third-party enters the negotiations for the purpose of helping the parties reach agreement. The mediator is "neutral" in the sense that he or she has no allegiance to either side and no interest in the outcome of the bargaining. In many instances, the mediator will be an employee of the Federal Mediation and Conciliation Service, a branch of the federal government, and provided at no cost to the parties. In some states, the state labor board will also assign mediators to assist in public sector negotiations. The mediator is selected either by agreement, by the terms of the existing contract, or by the laws of the jurisdiction in which the bargaining takes place. In IBB bargaining the mediator will generally have been working with the parties from the outset. Traditional bargaining, however, usually requires that the parties have reached impasse before mediation will begin.

Mediation is sometimes confused with arbitration, a process by which a third party resolves a dispute with a ruling that is binding on both sides. Mediation is far different in that the mediator does not decide anything. It is important to know, as many good mediators will make clear, that it's up to the parties to reach agreement—agreement won't be dictated by the mediator. The mediator can't and won't tell either side what to agree or disagree to, and success for the mediator is achieved when the parties reach agreement. Whether it's ultimately a good or bad agreement is up to the parties to decide. It's also important to understand that the mediator has no authority to require agreement on any issue. The mediator's authority is limited to the power to convene the parties. That said, a good mediator will quickly identify the "blocking" issues in the bargaining process and explore ways to overcome those issues with the parties.

Labor dispute mediation generally follows the same process as other types of mediation, such as domestic, civil disputes, and commercial dispute mediation. However, there are few real rules, and it generally falls to the individual mediator to determine how he or she wishes to proceed. The following describes what generally happens, but there are no guarantees that it will happen this way in any specific case.

In most cases, the mediator will initially convene the bargaining teams together for introduction and background purposes. Good labor mediators are very much in demand and, with the exception of IBB bargaining, the mediator will likely have no background on what's been going on in the negotiations before arriving on the scene. There are usually no written pre-bargaining memoranda or briefs submitted. After introductions, the mediator will meet separately with each bargaining team to learn their take on the outstanding issues. Here it's critical to understand that the mediator *will not share* information given in confidence by one team to the mediator. In order for mediation to be successful, the mediator has to understand the issues, including what concessions might be made by each side. Armed with that information, the mediator can begin to explore alternate solutions.

SIDEBARS AND SUPPOSALS

The mediator will often meet, either together or separately, with the chief negotiators for each side. All three of those individuals, assuming that neither chief negotiator is an employee of either party, have a common interest in achieving resolution of the bargaining impasse and in reaching ultimate agreement. Thus the issue discussion can occur without the emotion that often clouds the thinking of the individuals on the bargaining teams. Some mediators will offer their own ideas for resolution, often presented in the form of "supposals" such as, for example, "Suppose we spread the salary increase over the three years of the contract rather than implementing it all in the first year?" Since the mediator isn't a party to the negotiations, he or she can't "propose" anything but is simply asking the teams to react to a "what-if" idea. Yet, if agreement is close but neither side is willing to propose the "winning" solution, the mediator may offer it as a "mediator's proposal" and ask each team to consider it as though it had been made by the opposing party. The strategy often results in agreement.

PREPARING YOUR TEAM FOR MEDIATION

In some cases, mediation may well be the last stop between impasse and a union strike vote. In preparing for mediation, you should expect that the mediator will push both sides for concessions in an effort to find common ground for agreement. Your team should plan for mediation in advance of the actual mediation outside the presence of either the mediator or the other side. At the meeting, the mediation process should be described, and the team should consider each of the issues, identify the blocking issues, and consider what movement, either on an individual issue or by combining them together, might be made on your side. Expect to be tested by the mediator when management has taken positions or made demands for contract concessions not consistent with those of similar bargaining units in the area. You can also anticipate that the union's bargaining team will receive the same treatment from the mediator. Don't wait until you're in the middle of mediation to consider possible movement on your side—there simply won't be sufficient time to do it effectively. Plan in advance.

Mediation, even in traditional bargaining, will also engage individual team members. Most mediation sessions will be held with the mediator meeting separately with each bargaining team. One of the reasons for that is to enable the mediator to effectively gauge the consensus of the team as a whole. If a blocking issue is the result of the personal agenda of one team member and lacks the full support of the others, the mediator needs to know that in order to move negotiations forward. Individual team members should be encouraged to share their views with the mediator. And, if any of them have workable, creative solutions for those issues, they should be encouraged to share those as well.

MEDIATION STRATEGIES

As noted above, most mediators prefer to work with individual teams and shuttle proposals back and forth until an agreement is reached. Some, however, like to convene the entire group and have each team, or in some cases, a team member, propose a solution to some problematic issue in mediation. This can be a very dangerous situation for the team that's not prepared for it because the team member least prepared could, under pressure, propose something completely unworkable or unaffordable. On the other hand, the "pressure proposal" technique sometimes produces very novel ideas that bring closure to the issue. Individual mediators bring their own style to the process, and it's always a good idea for your bargaining team to gather intelligence about your mediator if you haven't worked with him or her before.

Mediation sessions often last a full day, sometimes more. The mediator will usually have a good sense of whether there's a deal to be had and how long it will take to get there. Often mediation will proceed well into the evening, and even the following morning. So long as the mediator senses that the parties are moving toward a deal, the mediation will continue as long as it can. Multiple mediation sessions are not uncommon, depending on whether there is movement.

During mediation, the focus of discussions often moves from the formal, written offer/acceptance mode of the traditional bargaining sessions to more verbal, "what-if" discussions. Thus, as a general matter, neither party is technically bound to mediation agreements. However, attempts at retrenchment, or "take backs" will generally ensure that mediation will fail and move ultimate agreement off to sometime in the future.

Mediation will force each side to objectively weigh the merit of its positions in negotiations against the alternatives available at that time. Remember, the parties have previously discussed these issues, often at some length prior to reaching impasse. Having reached impasse, it is clear that some movement, likely on the part of each side, is necessary to bring the negotiations to a successful conclusion. Experienced mediators can sense the issues upon which movement is necessary and the nature of the movement required to reach agreement. The mediator will explore that movement with each of the teams to locate the magic "middle ground" between the opposing positions that could result in agreement. Mediation is one of the critical points in negotiations where a proposal that might not have had any chance of success earlier could well be successful now. One of the primary reasons for that is the fact that unsuccessful mediation leaves the parties with fewer alternatives than they had before, and some of those alternatives are not very attractive. Remember, timing is everything.

Agreements reached in the course of mediation need to be reduced to writing as quickly as possible because the pace of discussions is often frenetic, and details can easily be lost, especially in the wee morning hours. The chief negotiators need to document the details as agreement is reached so that final agreements can be T/A'd before the session ends. It is often the case that a final mediation session will successfully resolve a wide range of outstanding issues—late at night after a long and difficult session. Team members on both sides will shake hands, congratulate each other, and head home for a well-deserved rest. Yet many of the resolutions were verbal only, and a final written agreement needs to be developed and signed by the chief negotiators. Disagreement about exactly what was agreed to in late-night mediation is not uncommon, and the potential for that should be anticipated and avoided where possible. Get it written down and agreed to by both sides before they leave the room.

When Mediation Fails

Mediation results in bringing the parties to agreement in the vast majority of cases, but not all of them. When mediation fails, the parties are faced with difficult decisions. First, the existing contract has expired or is close to expiration. Will the union agree to extend the contract for a period of time? Some unions steadfastly refuse to either extend the expiring contract or to continue to work without a new one. Such a position leaves the union no choice other than to declare a strike. We'll talk more about that later.[4] A far better choice is for the parties to recognize that they have obstacles to overcome before reaching agreement and to chart a course for overcoming those obstacles. That course may well include a short-term extension of the existing contract. Here are some of the other options that may be available or in some cases required to be followed.

OTHER STRATEGIES: FACT-FINDING

Some jurisdictions provide for the appointment of a fact-finding panel to review the positions of the parties and make a recommendation. I'm not a fan of "fact-finding" for several reasons. First, it's a misnomer. At least in Ohio, the panel doesn't see its role as one of determining disputed facts, rather, it sees its role as the decider of all of the remaining negotiations disputes. Usually, that decision falls somewhere near the mid-point of each side's last offer, thus forcing compromise neither side was willing to make in negotiations. My concern is that the fact-finders have no relationship to the community or the employees and no responsibility for the results of its award. In some cases, fact-finding recommendations become binding on the parties unless rejected by a super-majority vote of either side's membership. This favors management because its governing board is much smaller than the entire bargaining unit, thus requiring far fewer votes to reject a recommendation.[5] Fact-finding reports are generally made public, and each side wants to be viewed as the "winner" of the process by being able to claim that the fact-finder agreed with that side's position. At the point of impasse, public support takes on an increased level of significance in the process. In my experience, fact-finding has seldom served the parties very well, and I have tended to avoid it if possible.

BINDING INTEREST ARBITRATION

Another dispute resolution process is called binding interest arbitration. What it does is require the parties to submit the issues remaining in dispute to binding arbitration, with the result that the arbitration award becomes binding on both parties. Interest arbitration can take one of three possible formats: arbitration of each outstanding issue, arbitration that results in selecting the "last offer" of one of the parties on each outstanding issue, or arbitration that results in the selection of the entire "last offer package" of one side or the other.[6] The "interest arbitration" distinguishes the process from grievance arbitration, in which disputes arising under the agreed contract are submitted to an arbitrator for resolution. My advice is to avoid binding interest arbitration if at all possible. The reason is that the arbitrator is required to resolve issues that the parties have been unable to resolve for themselves. Yet, the arbitrator has no stake in the outcome of the process. If the arbitrator's wage determination bankrupts the enterprise, too bad. The arbitrator has no accountability for the result. Those who are accountable, the governing board or other governing authority, are left to deal with the damage.

Notwithstanding the potential adverse consequences, there are some circumstances in which binding interest arbitration is unavoidable, and if that consequence lies in the path of your bargaining, it is important to plan for it. Research is not only helpful, but essential. You need to know the history of the arbitrator's rulings in similar circumstances and the arguments that carry the most weight. Unless the arbitrator is required either by law or by agreement of the parties to select between the last offer made by one side or the other, there is a tendency to "split the difference" and land in or close to the mid-point between the two positions. If you know that is a likely result, you may want to plan your last offer accordingly.[7]

Unless the laws of your jurisdiction require binding interest arbitration as a dispute resolution strategy, I would never, ever agree to put it into the contract as a dispute resolution strategy. Likewise, if you are using binding interest arbitration as a "one-off" strategy, make it clear in the arbitration agreement that the arbitrator lacks authority to include binding interest arbitration in the contract for the resolution of future disputes as part of his or her award. Once a provision gets into contract, it is very, very hard to get it out.

At this point, most bargaining ventures have been resolved. Sometimes, however, it simply doesn't work as expected and the parties have failed to reach agreement. Now, the dynamics of power come much more to the fore, with each side exercising and threatening to further exercise the power that it has. For the union, the power relates to the delivery of labor; for management, the power relates to the control of the budget and the workplace. In the next chapter we will discuss a few of the more common interactions that take place between this point in your negotiations and the beginning of a strike.

CHAPTER 12

Late-Stage Bargaining Strategies

A t this point you have exhausted your dispute resolution process to no avail, bargaining remains at impasse, and further discussions seem unlikely to produce any change. Tensions are high, and the union is beginning to talk about a strike. What happens between now and the beginning of that strike is what we are referring to as "late-stage" bargaining. As with most other things in collective bargaining, there is no "set agenda" to define what will happen in your case. Rather, the following describes some of the things that unions and management have done when faced with similar circumstances in the past. They are offered to show what could happen, not what will or even should happen in your case.

Timing begins to play an even more important role. With no agreement, and no willingness to move by either side, further discussions are unlikely to bring progress. The absence of agreement, combined with the lack of negotiations injects a great deal of uncertainty for all of those with an interest in the outcome. In the school context, for example, parents will begin to wonder if school will happen. Teachers are faced with the possibility of dealing with a strike, and management is faced with the consequences of all of those possibilities. These forces increase with the passage of time and will, hopefully, force each side to further consider the merits of its positions on the blocking issues. It's important for the mediator and the chief negotiators for both sides to stay in touch and keep the door open for further negotiations.

The passage of time generally works to the benefit of management. Without a new agreement, management isn't paying any of the additional benefits that were sought by the union, even though they may have been tentatively agreed to in the course of negotiations.[1] Thus, union members are "losing money" by the day, and that fact tends to increase the pressure on the union to come to agreement. But, as the length of impasse grows, each side becomes increasingly "locked in" to the positions it has taken, and movement becomes more difficult. That's where the mediator can make a big difference.

As a neutral third party, the mediator can suggest proposals that neither side would be willing or able to make on its own, for fear of being labeled the side that "blinked' in negotiations. Yet, it becomes increasingly clear that something new is needed to move the parties forward. Sometimes that means nothing more than having a new individual join the negotiations team, a new location for discussions, or a new idea about how to resolve the blocking issues. The key factor is for the chief negotiators on each side to remain in communication, both with each other and, hopefully, with the mediator.

MANAGEMENT'S LAST, BEST OFFER

Another term of art, the "last, best offer" is a bargaining strategy sometimes used by management in late-stage negotiations.[2] The concept is simply this: at some point, management is going to be required to make the best offer that it is prepared to make to resolve the negotiations. When that offer is made, it has nothing left to offer and no reason to continue to engage in what then becomes meaningless discussions with the union. When the "last, best" offer is presented, the union has no choice other than to accept the offer, go on strike in hopes of forcing a better offer, or simply go back to work without a contract. Making a "last, best" offer is problematic for management because, if not accepted, it has no other moves to make. Changing its position after making a "last, best" would mean that its "last, best" wasn't either the last or the best, and the loss of credibility will haunt management in future negotiations.

Apart from the strategic implications of making a "last, best offer," management must be certain that it has actually fulfilled all of its good-faith collective bargaining obligations and has no legal obligation to continue bargaining. If management intends to implement its last, best offer it also needs to be sure that it can legally do so. Be very, very careful about making a last, best offer.

UNION STRATEGIES WHEN MEDIATION FAILS

Recall the earlier comments about timing? It may mean that the parties just aren't ready to reach agreement yet. In that instance it may be far better for the parties to simply adjourn negotiations for a while so that both sides can better assess their positions. Just because no formal bargaining sessions are happening doesn't mean that other, more complex strategies won't be going on. The union has a range of strategies that it might employ to pressure management toward agreement. On the surface, these strategies are used in an effort to convince management to change its position on the blocking issues. However, that seldom works, and union leadership fully understands that. The underlying purpose of the strategies is to build solidarity among the members of the bargaining unit in the event that the union believes that a strike is necessary. We don't suggest that any of these strategies would be used in any particular negotiations, but because they have so often been used in the past, they are worth mentioning here. Here is a brief listing of some of those strategies, simply to prepare you in the event they are utilized. There is no particular order of preference that I'm aware of.

PUBLIC CRITICISM. Because public sector governing boards are often either elected or appointed officials, they are viewed as being vulnerable to public pressure. Unions have utilized various techniques to publicize the (in their view) unfairness of management in not reaching agreement on the union's bargaining issues. These techniques include writing letters to the editor, social media postings, and massive union membership attendance at governing board meetings, with all union members wearing colorful T-shirts emblazoned with their negotiations complaints. Calls to individual governing board members are often included in this strategy, all in an effort to build support for the union's position.

STRIKE VOTE. Unions are democratic organizations, each with their own rules about how they will deal with strike authorization. However, a vote of some sort is almost always necessary, and while an affirmative strike vote "authorizes" a work stoppage, it doesn't necessarily mean that a strike will happen. You will likely never know if the union took a strike vote that failed, but if the strike vote passed, it will become well-publicized information. And, while the union's passing a strike vote is more a bargaining tool than harbinger of a strike, don't ever assume that a strike won't happen.

ADVERTISING. Earlier we described the confidentiality rules that govern many public sector collective bargaining activities. But, at this point in bargaining, many of those rules are stretched to the maximum as the union begins to publicize its complaints about the management's failure to agree. Newspaper ads, newsletters, social media comments, and other forms of advertising are sometimes used at this stage. Often, the public lament is characterized more in the mantle of "unfairness" or "bad-faith" accusations rather than disclosure of specific proposals or counterproposals, though those too can become fair game. In response, management will be pressured to publicly respond in kind and if it does, the rhetoric of the dispute will escalate. The dilemma for management is often that it believes its bargaining proposals have been entirely reasonable in light of the union's demands. But it is prohibited by the confidentiality rules from publicly disclosing what went on at the bargaining table. Despite the desire to respond tit for tat to the union's rhetoric, I believe the better approach is not to get into the mud, but to maintain a position of openness to reasonable settlement at any time.

ULPS. Most states that authorize public sector collective bargaining have some form of labor board with authority to hear and determine claims of wrongdoing by either side in the course of bargaining. Unfair labor practice charges are often brought by one side or the other at this stage of bargaining, and sometimes by both sides. The charges can run the gamut from "bad-faith" bargaining to unlawful "direct dealing" with union members through management publications or other communications. As a practical matter, by the time an unfair labor practice charge is heard and resolved, the parties will have long since settled bargaining, but the publicity value of the charges makes them attractive measures at the time they are filed.

INFORMATIONAL PICKETING. While picketing is normally thought of as a strike activity, informational picketing, especially at the homes or places of business of governing board members ,is another technique used by unions in this circumstance. Again, the twin goals are to bring pressure on the governing board members as well as to build solidarity among the bargaining unit membership.

WORK-TO-RULE. Most public-sector employees routinely do far more than their work rules actually require. For example, teachers go far out of their way to meet with parents, tutor students, and attend school functions after hours. Likewise, non-teaching employees often do far more than the minimum necessary for the job. However, at this juncture, they will be told by the union to engage in a concerted effort to do no more than the minimum required until negotiations are resolved.

Depending on the circumstances, "work-to-rule" can be a very effective pressure technique because it puts additional pressure on the managers—those who would be most directly impacted in the event of a strike.

BLUE FLU. Even though paid absences from work are highly regulated in the public sector, sick calls, though recorded, are seldom verified. It's not uncommon for the incidence of absences from work due to claims of illness to spike markedly. The employer generally has the burden of proving that the request for paid sick leave is unjustified, and it seldom has the resources to pursue that sort of claim. As a result, attendance lags, services decline, and labor costs increase due to the need for substitutes. Blue Flu epidemics can exert tremendous pressure on management.

MANAGEMENT RESPONSES

It is important to understand that the wide range of circumstances that can accompany a collective bargaining impasse makes it impossible to formulate a "one-fits-all" management response to any one or more of the union strategies. The governing board needs to consult its labor counsel and carefully consider the advice given. My personal responses to these strategies have been to advise management to develop and maintain a public position emphasizing the following points:

- "We are ready to return to the bargaining table at any time if it appears that progress toward resolving the impasse could be made."
- "We are charged with the management of public tax

dollars and must use those responsibly. While we regret the union's disagreement with our decisions, we make them in light of the broader interest."

- "We expect our employees to honor their employment obligations, both during and after bargaining."

Many governing board members, being the political folk they often are, feel compelled to respond to the union's publicity barrage, which is often filled with inaccuracies begging to be corrected. However, that's not always the best strategy. Remember that the public expects responsible governance, and for management to engage in public debate with its union over wages and benefit issues often portrays an image of panic rather than certitude. While it's hard to resist the urge to publicly respond, sometimes minimal response, or none at all, is best. Moreover, public posturing about negotiation positions simply adds grist to the "unfair labor-practice mill" that may well be grinding out new charges filed by the union at this stage of the negotiations.

STRIKE PLANNING

Another late-stage measure for management is strike planning, which is often governed by individual state laws and regulations, the details of which are beyond the scope of this work.[3] However, strike planning is necessary, even if you want to believe that the strike will never happen. The fact that it *could* happen is sufficient to trigger serious consideration of some of the critical issues, the first of which is whether to attempt to remain open for the delivery of services, or to close the enterprise for the duration of the strike. Remaining open will necessarily involve reassigning management staff to other duties and likely will also involve recruiting short-term substitutes ("scabs") to stand in for striking workers. Strikes are more problematic in the public sector than in the private sector because the mission of the enterprise is to serve the public, and interruption of that service is harmful on a widespread scale. That is why many states prohibit strikes by safety forces bargaining units.

Not only is strike planning important for management, it is equally important that the union know that strike planning is taking place, particularly when management is planning to maintain operations during the strike. One of the strategic reasons for maintaining operations during a strike is the fact that the economic pressure on the union is far greater if it knows that the withholding of services by the bargaining unit members won't prevent, at least entirely, the delivery of services by the enterprise. In that event, the potential for a long strike, with accompanying long-term loss of wages and benefits by union members, becomes a significant factor in the calculation. What follows is a brief list of some of the essential preparations for management contemplating a possible strike:

- If you haven't done so already, secure experienced legal counsel to help develop and implement your strike plan.
- Secure all essential keys, access cards, passwords, service manuals, schedules, routes, and directories currently in the hands of potentially striking employees.
- Increase the security of your facilities.
- Alert local law enforcement to the potential for a strike and potential disruptions.

- Prepare to document and record acts of disruption by striking workers.
- Secure your computer systems from potential hacking.
- Prepare a list of available substitutes and plan to convey them safely to and from the work site through picket lines.
- Plan for the safe access of members of the public to your facilities, and prepare for immediate legal action if the safety of any member of the public is jeopardized by the strike activity.

Successfully maintained operation during a strike can have a devastating impact on the union, as further discussed in the next chapter. If the enterprise believes that it can maintain operations, I would let that fact be known to the membership before the strike happens, in hopes that it may cause a change in bargaining position.

Finally, be prepared for a long night of bargaining as the strike deadline approaches. Many potential strikes are resolved at the last minute when the union leadership can truly say that they have achieved all that they could achieve in bargaining, and management can truly say that they have done all they can to fairly and economically resolve negotiations. If the strike deadline is midnight, the "magic moment" is 11:59 p.m. I've seen a lot of potential strikes resolved at just that moment. If you haven't made that "last offer" yet, that will be the time.

CHAPTER 13

Strike!

Just as war is a failure of diplomacy, strikes are a failure of bargaining. Failures happen. It is important to note that not all public sector bargaining includes the right to strike. This chapter assumed that the union has the right to strike and has fulfilled all of the necessary conditions to exercise that right. We assume that all of the dispute resolution efforts have failed, the strike deadline has passed, and employees are picketing in front of the building rather than reporting for work. Now, what do you do? The first and most important thing to understand is that strikes are bad. Strikes are bad for both sides, and the collateral damage from a strike can spread far and last for decades. There are many victims to consider, and it is important to understand the dynamics of harm wrought by a strike.

First, consider the employees and their families. The decision to report to the picket line rather than reporting to work is gut-wrenching for many employees who are forced to choose between loyalty to their job and loyalty to their union. Choosing the picket line means a loss of wages and benefits for them and their families. The longer the strike lasts, the less chance they will ever recoup those lost wages through the pay increase they are striking to gain. On the other hand, crossing the picket line and reporting to work means rejecting their colleagues, forever being labeled a "scab," and being ostracized at the workplace after the strike is over. The damage to work relationships, which can cut deep and last for years, can significantly change the nature of the work environment in the future.

Strikes are equally difficult for management, now forced to more than double-duty to maintain some semblance of operations in the face of striking employee hostility. Principals, administrators, and supervisors are now thrust into an adversarial role with their employees as they cross the picket line to go to work. Likewise, the governing board is faced with mounting public concern and often criticism as the strike lengthens. They have made critical choices, presumably based on the best interests of the enterprise, that are now being challenged by the strike.

The enterprise's clientele is also a victim, most dramatically in the case of a school strike, where pupils must cross their teacher's picket line to attend classes taught by ill-prepared substitutes or stay home and receive no education. Though online instruction may now be an option for some, the quality of instruction during a strike likely won't be any better. The ultimate losers in school strikes are the pupils whose education is impaired or interrupted for no valid reason. Strikes in other aspects of public service can be equally devastating, as services are delayed or withheld from those most in need of them.

While strikes are a poor bargaining strategy, public-sector unions have few other options, and if they can't achieve their goals any other way, they sometimes believe they are forced to that choice. However, in my experience, strikes are the result of a failure of the bargaining process on one or both sides of the table and could have been avoided had bargaining been done better.

MANAGEMENT STRIKE PLAN

As noted earlier, whenever it appears that a strike is being seriously considered by the union, management needs to develop and prepare to implement a comprehensive strike plan. Help can often be found from similar public sector enterprises that have faced strikes, or the threat of strikes, the statewide support organization, if your state has one, or from experienced labor counsel. Here are some of the primary goals of that plan:

- Secure the safety of the public, the enterprise's clients, and the employees who will continue working during the strike.
- Continue the operation of the enterprise's services during the strike to the fullest extent possible.
- Retain and deploy a sufficient level of temporary staff to continue services.
- Channel strike-related communications from and to the enterprise through a single point, such as the chief operating officer, governing board president, or public relations designee.
- Make the striking workers aware that they are welcome to return to work, if that is management's position.
- Assure the public that services will continue to be provided, if that is the case.
- Record and document the conduct of striking workers

in the event that litigation becomes necessary to limit or halt picketing activity.

- Consider retention of a public relations consultant to assist with strike-related communications.

Maintaining operations involves having a workforce, usually including management employees who are not part of the bargaining unit as well as temporary workers recruited for strike duty. Some services will recruit and provide such employees for strike service but at a hefty price.

If management has not already done so, one of the first things to do is retain experienced labor counsel to advise it on the defense of the strike. Every action taken by management during the strike will have significant legal implications for the enterprise, and missteps can be extremely costly. Here's just one real-life example. The enterprise provides health insurance for bargaining unit members and their families. The group insurance premium was due the second day of the strike. The CFO, not wanting to pay benefits to striking workers, canceled health insurance coverage for all of those on strike, unaware of prior notice requirements that had to be met. Unfortunately, one of the striking bargaining unit members had a family member undergoing open heart surgery at the same time. The insurance company refused to pay, and of course, lawsuits followed. The untimely cancellation of insurance benefits became a costly mistake for management that could have been avoided.

While the use of temporary employees is a fairly common management strategy during a strike, the replacement of striking workers with new, permanent employees, is generally not available as a strategy in the public sector. If employees have a legal right to strike in your jurisdiction, the loss of their job in order to exercise that right is generally prohibited. On the other hand, potential job loss would, if available, become an enormous disincentive to a strike. Consult your legal counsel regarding the laws in effect in your state to determine your options.

USING THE COURTS

Strikes are emotional events, on both sides of the dispute. Emotions can easily get out of control and become violent. Picketing, jostling, yelling insults, and epithets are common occurrences in the early days of a strike. Management's primary interest at this point is the welfare of its employees, the welfare of the public, and the enterprise's clients, and if it's a school, the safety of its pupils. Additionally, management needs to secure the property it controls from damage, which can also happen during a strike. Given these considerations, two questions need to be addressed on an ongoing basis. First, is the conduct of the striking workers and their supporters threatening the welfare of non-striking employees, clients, members of the public, or pupils? Second, is the conduct threatening the security of public property under the control of the enterprise? If the answer to either of these is "yes," consider seeking injunctive relief in court.

If judges are elected in your jurisdiction, remember that the union likely has a lot more votes than management. At the same time, there are usually a lot more voting taxpayers than union members. Indisputable evidence of unlawful conduct representing a threat to the welfare of others is hard to ignore. That evidence is best captured on video as well as by personal testimony. Keep the video records of strike activity handy if there is any chance you may be seeking judicial relief.

DETERMINE THE COST

Putting aside the emotions, the issues giving rise to the strike can be reduced to a dollar cost, and it is important for both sides to consider that cost. For management, a daily cost estimate can be made by considering the additional cost of the benefit, wage, or other issues causing the strike on a per diem basis together with the additional costs of strike personnel, litigation, and other related strike costs minus the wages and benefits not paid. For the union side, the cost is the daily value of the benefit, wage, or other issues they are striking to achieve minus the daily value of the wages and benefits lost by reason of the strike. Knowing these numbers will not necessarily cause the strike to end any earlier than it would otherwise end, but it will provide additional incentive to settle when the time is right.

STRIKE TIMING

Strikes take on a life of their own, and there are some critical stages to that life. The first is the "final-hours" bargaining, which often avoids the strike altogether. If that fails, the next stage is during the first three to five days when the union finds out how many of the employees will really support the strike, refuse to report for work, and report for duty on the picket line. If the union believes that despite what they said, a sufficient number of employees will not support the strike, it will quickly look for alternatives to resolve the dispute. Likewise, the governing board may discover that public sentiment heavily favors the striking employees, and be forced to reconsider its position on the strike issues.

The next pressure point is the passage of the first payday after the strike. Now, the employees are faced with the harsh reality of lost income and potential loss of health insurance as well. Some will do the math and realize the true cost of the strike when compared with the potential gain from the issues they are striking over. One of the harsh realities of strikes is that employees seldom gain any real benefit, and the longer the strike goes on, the more they lose. Beyond the initial fifteen or so days, strikes become a war of attrition, with public relations strategies becoming increasingly important. Public sentiment for or in opposition to the strike can have a significant impact on how long it will last.

In my experience, once a strike has gone beyond the initial stages, it will tend to continue until something changes. The change could be a small one, such as a minor tweak to a proposal, or a change in bargaining team membership or bargaining location, but there needs to be a reason for the negotiating teams to reconvene and try again.

MANAGING THE STRIKE

Once the strike commences, bargaining generally ceases until something changes. It is highly unlikely that either side will send up the white flag and concede defeat. Rather, backchannel messages are sent, usually through the mediator, that it's time to take another look at the issues and explore possibilities for resolution. Until that happens, management's greatest challenge is one of assuring the public that it is looking after their welfare, continuing to provide services, securing public property, and standing ready to return to the bargaining table and resolve the strike whenever there is a reasonable opportunity to do so. Public relations becomes paramount.

Two numbers should be on speed-dial during the strike: the public relations consultant, if any, hired to help with strike communications, and the governing board's attorney. If a public relations professional isn't used, someone on the management side should be designated as the PR contact person. Public employee strikes are news media events, and the information coming from the management side should be carefully managed to control public perception of the event.

MAKING PEACE

All strikes end sometime. Reopening negotiations and reaching tentative agreement on a final package is the first part of ending the strike. Dismissal of all of the ULPs and any other litigation filed before and during the strike is another part. As noted earlier, the emotional carnage to employees, labor, and management alike that can flow from a strike can last for many years. For example, teachers who crossed the picket line and worked during the strike may be singled out for retaliation by their peers. Elected board members may be faced with voter disapproval if the strike is viewed as the fault of management. Likewise, the superintendent or chief manager is often on the short-list for replacement regardless of the outcome of the strike. Faced with these realities it's hard for both sides to simply "forgive and forget" about the strike. But that's the essence of what's necessary to move on.

Unions often demand "no retaliation" provisions in the agreement as a condition of settling a strike. Since, in many states, public employers are already barred from retaliating against employees for lawful strike activity anyway, the inclusion of such a provision is often redundant for management. But consider adding a "no retaliation" commitment on the part of the union as well.

One idea for easing the transition is the periodic use of a labor-management council, a committee of employees and managers, often facilitated by a neutral third party to provide a forum for the airing and resolution of retaliation issues, at least for a while. Whether or not you look for palliative measures, management should be prepared for fallout after the strike ends.

In the next chapter we talk about ratification, both by the union and by management, as well as learning to live with the new contract. Keep in mind that negotiations are never really over until ratification takes place.

CHAPTER 14

Agreement and Beyond

Once all of the negotiations issues have been either tentatively agreed to, withdrawn, or otherwise disposed of to the joint satisfaction of the bargaining teams, it is tempting to pop the champagne corks, congratulate each other, and move on to the next challenge. But there is still a great deal of work to be done. In this chapter we talk about agreements, ratification, learning to live with the new contract, and yes, in some cases, the potential for still more negotiations.

HOW TO SAY "YES"

Every negotiation ends, and in most cases, it ends with the parties having reached tentative agreement on all of the issues. The final "yes" usually involves the most important issue or package of issues, usually monetary, and often takes place after a sidebar conference over the water cooler. The final "yes" also involves all or nearly all the concessions either side is willing to make. I have consistently advised bargaining clients to never put the "last dime" (being the last concession on the last issue) on the table until they know that it will get a deal. Of course, the only way to know that in advance is through informal sidebar discussions, but by this point some level of trust has been created or the discussions wouldn't be happening in the first place. One strategy I like to use is to try to get the union to make the last offer, knowing informally that it will likely be accepted. That gives the union the credit for making the deal, but it also prevents them from backing away when management says yes to *their* offer. Of course, a brief management caucus is necessary before accepting the offer, if only to add dramatic flavor.

RATIFICATION

Ratification is the last stop in the approval process and happens only when both sides (union/enterprise) have agreed, by formal action of their membership, in the case of the union, and governing board, in the case of the enterprise, to all of the terms of the new contract. Since what is being voted on is the entire agreement, it is generally necessary to submit all of the provisions of that agreement, including the carried-over language from the old contract as well as the agreed language of the new provisions for approval. In some cases, only summaries are actually distributed to union members due to the length and complexity of the document. As a matter of custom and practice, the union votes on the final package first, and the governing board votes after union approval. The ratification vote should take place as soon as possible after the final tentative agreement by the bargaining teams. Delaying the ratification vote can have some negative consequences for both sides; the "rumor mill" will start to spread sometimes erroneous information about the tentative agreement among union members, and that can poison the chances of ratification. In some states, the press may seek disclosure of the yet-confidential final tentative agreement as a public record. Disclosure before the ratification vote is never a good idea.

It is vitally important for the bargaining teams, especially the lead negotiators, to make sure that the document that goes to the union and governing board for ratification reflects the agreement of the bargaining teams and that both sides are voting on identical provisions. As noted earlier, and especially after a late-night final mediation session, it's not uncommon for one side to believe that an issue has been resolved in one way and the other side believe it has been resolved in a different way, only to later discover that each side has ratified a contract with different language. That's a problem that could have been avoided if the parties had taken the time to prepare and jointly review a final document representing the end result of negotiations and submitted the same document to each side for ratification.

The process of reaching tentative agreement on a proposal in bargaining carries with it two representations: first, that the bargaining team approves the proposal and, second, that the bargaining team will recommend it to its principal (union or governing board) for ratification. In some cases, the union bargaining team is willing to agree to the first part but unwilling to go on record recommending the final package to its membership. Here the union team may offer to "take it to a vote." In other words, to agree on the final package and take the entire package to a vote of its membership, but without the affirmative recommendation of the bargaining team. I'm not a fan of this strategy. What's bargained for is both agreement and the recommendation, and anything less, to me, is not an agreement at all. Further, it carries with it the implicit message to the union membership that they might get a better deal by turning down the tentative package. Keep in mind that a ratification vote is to either approve or disapprove the entire contract; it is not a vote on any specific provision of that contract.

RATIFICATION ... OR NOT

Ratification is, generally, the success story in bargaining. The teams have reached tentative agreement on all outstanding bargaining issues, and the package of agreements has been assembled for ratification by the union and governing board. So, what could possibly go wrong? Well, sometimes, lots.

One of the primary concerns is what happens when the union turns down the tentative agreement. In current times, union rejection of a contract package is not at all uncommon, and when it happens it presents both union leadership and management with a difficult set of circumstances. Rejection usually means that the union membership believes that there's a better deal to be had. Yet, it's fair to assume that management spent all of the money and made all of the concessions it was willing to make to get to that tentative agreement and that it is unwilling to spend more money or to make more concessions. Both sides now have a problem: if management sweetens the deal to get ratification, it will lose credibility in future negotiations, having now created a precedent for sweetening the deal after union rejection. At the same time, the union's bargaining team has lost credibility. When the team negotiates an agreement in good faith only to have it rejected by vote of the membership, management can rightly question whether it has been bargaining with the right people.

Management should do what it can to discourage rejection of a tentative agreement by the union as a bargaining practice. Unless there is some reason not to, I'd suggest a long hiatus before returning to the bargaining table after a final tentative agreement has been turned down by the union—to provide time for the union membership to reconsider their decision should they wish to do so. When bargaining does resume, the management posture should be one of "moving the chairs on the deck," i.e. massaging items already agreed to rather than making new, different sorts of concessions in an effort to reach agreement. When it becomes clear that the initial deal agreed to by the bargaining team is the best alternative, some [very] slightly modified version of that deal can again be submitted for ratification, and it will likely be approved.

Governing board rejection of a tentative agreement is even rarer, but it also happens. Unlike union rejection, governing board failure to ratify takes place, generally, *after* the union has ratified the tentative agreement. Failure to ratify, in this instance, signals a fundamental communications failure between the governing board and its bargaining team. If the team has agreed to a provision that is *so* offensive to the governing board as to bar ratification, the team has failed its mission, unless, of course, the governing board never told them.

Going forward from a governing board rejection is difficult for management for the same reasons as for the union.

The bargaining team has lost credibility. There is no longer assurance that any further agreements approved by the team will be ratified. In addition, the most likely reasoning for the rejection is that the team agreed to "too much" of something in the package and that the size of the package (benefits or otherwise) must now be reduced in order for the governing board to approve it the next time around. Such regressive bargaining is symptomatic of bad faith and, in any event, puts both the governing board and its management structure in a very bad light. Fortunately, I've never had that happen. If it did, the first step would be to make sure the governing board fully understood the consequences of its action, and plan, hopefully, for reconsideration.

Consider the Public Relations Opportunity

Though generally not required either by law or practice, it's a good idea for both management and labor to issue a press release announcing the successful conclusion of negotiations. After all, the real interested parties, the taxpayers, need to be reassured that services will continue without labor strife and, hopefully, that their taxes won't go up to make that happen.

If a press release is issued, be careful to make it a joint union/management release and avoid going into much detail about the terms of the settlement, especially when the agreement hasn't yet been ratified by both sides. Too much detail could diminish the chances of ratification.

POST-BARGAINING STRATEGIES

A good idea for management, though seldom implemented in my experience, is to have a meeting with each of the managers responsible for implementing the "new" contract and review it with them to be sure that they understand what's expected. It's amazing how often costly and time-consuming grievances arise simply because a manager didn't know or understand what was required under the labor agreement.

Whether part of the contract or not, periodic labor-management meetings to review the operation of the new contract are also a good idea. First, regular labor-management communications can provide a safety valve to release internal pressures that may be building in the workplace and, second, such meetings can go far to avoid costly grievances and other workplace disputes.

MEMORANDA OF UNDERSTANDING

It is not uncommon for questions to come up during the administration of a contract about the meaning of a particular provision, or how that provision will be applied. For example, the contract provides for ten days of paid vacation per year for bargaining unit members but fails to specify exactly when that vacation leave becomes available. Past practice has credited vacation leave on the anniversary of each bargaining unit member's employment, but the administration of the provision has not been uniform. Both parties want clarification, but the current contract doesn't come up for negotiation for two years. In that circumstance, the parties might want to consider a memorandum of understanding

(MOU), a formal document that sets forth the agreement about how the vacation leave accrual issue will be handled, an agreement signed by the union president and the chief executive officer of the enterprise and attached to (but not part of) the negotiated agreement. The MOU documents the verbal agreement but is not part of the union contract because it was not negotiated and not ratified. Such memoranda are commonly used in the administration of public-sector union contracts.

EFFECTS BARGAINING

After ratification by both sides, the collective bargaining agreement becomes a legally binding contract that is in effect for the period of time stated in the contract. There is, generally, no obligation to bargain again on any issue until it's time to bargain for the renewal of the contract. However, there are some circumstances in which bargaining during the term of an existing contract can be required.

Here's how that could work: If your state law defines the mandatory subjects of bargaining by statute, for example, "… wages, hours, and terms and conditions of employment…" the statute creates the framework for what can be bargained. Within that framework, the enterprise has all of the management rights, limited only by the terms of the collective bargaining agreement. However, when management makes a decision that affects the terms and conditions of employment for bargaining unit members, the union may have the right to bargain, not about the decision itself, but about the effects of that decision on its members. In one case, a university adopted an executive order that changed certain aspects of the curriculum for some students, and also imposed substantial additional record-keeping requirements on faculty. The union sought to negotiate the impacts, not of the order itself, but on the faculty. The California State Public Employment Relations Board held that the employer's refusal was unlawful and directed negotiations, but only on the "effects" of the order on the faculty working conditions.[1]

The "effects" bargaining issue is further complicated by the fact that public sector employment is governed by state law, not the National Labor Relations Board. While "effects" bargaining is generally required in the private sector, the same result is not necessarily true in the public sector as state law is widely varied. However, it is important to be aware of the issue and the potential for future bargaining, even after the contract has been agreed to.

GOING FORWARD – MISTAKES TO AVOID AND NUGGETS TO KEEP

The mistakes we're talking about here are the ones that can ultimately lead (or may have led) the parties to strike. Here are a few I've observed over time.

- Union-busting management style. When management displays an open hostility to all things union and takes measures to limit the union's power to act on behalf of its members, the relationship can and usually will sour to the point of open hostility in bargaining. Strikes of this sort are often long and acrimonious.
- Management publication of benefit cuts without bargaining. Unions jealously protect their right to bargain

the contract. When management publicly announces specific cuts or changes in terms and conditions of employment without bargaining or even recognizing the obligation to bargain, it waves a red flag in front of the union and generally creates an unnecessary backlash.

- The establishment of unreasonable management bargaining objectives. This is the most common and most dangerous mistake management can make. New governing board members often have specific ideas about what's wrong with the union contract—and how to fix it. What they often fail to realize is the current union contract is the result of bargaining—often multiple rounds of bargaining that took place before they came to the governing board. While they are free to seek change, those changes come with a price, and they need to understand that price before making changes a part of the agenda. Labor counsel with experience bargaining similar contracts in the area will have some understanding of the importance of issues to the union and, concurrently, the cost of changing those issues.

- Bargaining without legal counsel. Somewhat analogous to wandering blindfolded in a minefield, bargaining without counsel is foolish and dangerous. No private sector enterprise with an annual budget anywhere close to the size of your public enterprise would ever consider negotiating its largest and most costly contract without counsel. The belief that you are saving money is a false assumption. The most costly mistakes are made because of either bad language drafting or bad strategic choices—things that counsel could have helped avoid.

- Failure to understand the cost. Costly bargaining proposals can come in many forms, and the full cost is often hidden in the details. I once consulted with a school district in a nearby state that was essentially bankrupt because it had agreed to a union retirement benefits proposal without fully understanding what the proposal would cost. Instead of doing their own costing, they simply accepted the union's representation of what the benefit would cost—a number that turned out to be grossly understated. While it may be difficult to establish the true cost of many of the union's benefit proposals, it is absolutely critical that management understand the magnitude of that cost before agreeing. There simply is no "do-over" when you find out the true price tag.

Now that you understand the bargaining process, it is time to consider the substance of some of the more common bargaining issues. Keep in mind that in your state, the scope of potential bargaining issues may well be defined by state law. However, the contents of your current contract and bargaining history may also define the scope of available issues. Within these broad boundaries, the range of issues that might be included in a collective bargaining agreement is virtually unlimited, and the same provision can be described differently from one contract to another. In Part II we will review some of the more common contract provisions, with a brief discussion of how each provision works, and the interests of both the union and management in that provision.

CHAPTER 15

A Review of Some Common Contract Provisions

Early in our discussion we suggested that you read the negotiated agreement currently in place between your enterprise and its union, or if no agreement is in place, an agreement between a similar enterprise in your locality and its union. Some of the provisions you read are self-explanatory, others are not. In this section we will review a number of provisions found in nearly all collective bargaining agreements and describe why they are there, what they are intended to accomplish, and some aspects that may be problematic. For each of the topics there will be a general description of the union's and management's interests in that provision, as well as some issues to avoid if possible.

The terminology and descriptions used in collective bargaining agreements can vary widely from place to place, and you may find provisions described in terms that are different from the descriptions used here. Regardless of the descriptors, the intent of the provisions will be essentially the same. In light of the infinite diversity of issues found in collective bargaining agreements, what follows is an overview only, focused on the most critical issues, rather than an effort to comprehensively review all possible provisions. For each provision discussed, we have included a sample in the Appendix, drawn for a collective bargaining agreement to give you a look at what these provisions can look like in real life. As you review the Appendix provisions, keep in mind that they are the result of actual bargaining and often contain language that we would not have recommended if we were writing on a clean slate from a management prospective. That's what happens in real life.

RECOGNITION

Regardless of how it's described, most contracts include a provision by which the employer recognizes the union as the exclusive representative of a group of employees for collective bargaining purposes. That group of employees, collectively, makes up the bargaining unit. Employees in the bargaining unit enjoy the benefits of and are bound by the negotiated agreement; those not in the bargaining unit are not subject to the agreement. The recognition clause serves two purposes: first, to give official status to the union as the *exclusive bargaining representative* for the unit employees, and second, to identify the employees who make up that bargaining unit. The bargaining unit is described not by identifying the individuals in the unit, but by the job positions included in the unit. For example, a unit consisting of all of the school bus drivers and cooks would be described as all of the school bus drivers and cooks in the school district, rather than by naming the individuals currently in the bargaining unit.

Bargaining status can be acquired by a union in several ways, depending on the history of the enterprise and the laws governing public sector bargaining in the jurisdiction. Selection by vote of the employees is one way; voluntary recognition by the employer is another, and yet another is simply being "grandfathered" because it has historically been "the union." Here we assume the union has recognition, regardless of how it acquired that status.

Bargaining unit definition can be troublesome for management because, unless specifically provided otherwise, all employees who are in the bargaining unit are entitled to all of the benefits in the collective bargaining agreement, regardless of union membership. This can raise difficult questions. For example, if all bus drivers are in the unit, is a part-time bus driver, a substitute bus driver, or a probationary bus driver entitled to the same benefits as a regular full-time bus driver? These issues are best dealt with when the bargaining unit is first identified because subsequent changes in bargaining unit description that result in employees being either brought into or excluded from the bargaining unit are difficult negotiation subjects and should be avoided whenever possible. While the union is sometimes amenable to changes that would increase membership, it generally opposes changes that result in reducing membership. Another union concern is that, in many states, the status of "exclusive bargaining representative" carries with it the duty to represent the interests of all of the bargaining unit members, and excluding them from the bargaining unit is inconsistent with that obligation. Many of these issues can also be addressed within the contract by qualifying benefit provisions to apply, for example, on a pro rata basis for part-time employees or to exclude probationary employees from the protection of certain provisions such as discipline, dismissal, and grievance provisions until they have successfully completed the probationary period.[1]

UNION INTERESTS. First and foremost, the union wants to continue being the union. Its goal is to have as many dues-paying members as possible, and that interest is furthered by having the bargaining unit as large as possible in hopes the unit members will join the union and pay dues.[2] Beyond that, the union wants the ability to effectively represent its members. To that end, it may seek such things as advance notice of governing board meeting agendas and periodic labor-management meetings with operations supervisors.

MANAGEMENT INTERESTS. First, management needs a clear and concise definition of who's in and who's out of the unit. Managers, supervisors, and employees with the duty to assign, evaluate, hire, or fire unit members should not be part of the unit. Second, management needs to exclude those who, due to the nature of their work schedules, duties, or employment arrangement should not be entitled to all of the benefits of the negotiated agreement. Remember, whoever is "in the bargaining unit" is entitled to all of the benefits of the agreement, unless provisions are made to exclude or limit their participation. Temporary or substitute employees should not have the same job security and transfer rights as regular, full-time employees. But, if included in the bargaining unit, they will at least have a claim to those benefits, unless expressly limited or excluded.

WHAT TO AVOID. Try to avoid vague unit definitions that include highly specialized, technical positions. For example, a unit definition that includes "IT personnel" in a unit that also includes school district cooks and bus drivers may not serve you well in the future if the market for these employees becomes highly competitive and candidates are unwilling to work for negotiated union-scale wages and benefits. In addition, be sure to exclude employees exercising management duties, such as the authority to hire fire, assign, evaluate, or discipline from the bargaining unit.

A sample recognition provision is found at App. 1.

GRIEVANCE PROCEDURE

Every collective bargaining agreement will have a grievance procedure, though they may look vastly different from one another. The grievance procedure is the "complaint desk" for the bargaining unit, and the terms of that provision define the scope of remedies available to members who believe that their contract rights have been violated. The procedure is generally only available to employees who are members of the bargaining unit covered by the agreement, regardless of whether or not they are union members. It applies to the processing of "grievances" as defined in the agreement. In practice, the grievance procedure can be applied to everything from shop floor disputes to major contract interpretation issues. In many respects, it's one of the most important provisions in the contract, and volumes could be written documenting all of the various disputes that have become the subject of grievances.

WHAT TO LOOK FOR. There are three key questions to be answered as you review the grievance procedure: First, how is a grievance defined for purposes of the contract? The definition is critical and should ideally be limited only to conduct alleged to be a violation of the negotiated agreement. This is important because the definition frames the scope of issues that can be raised and resolved in the grievance procedure. For example, some contracts broadly define conduct that could be a grievance to include "unfair treatment" or "workplace discrimination," both of which are extremely broad and vague terms, suggesting that a grievance could be brought simply because an employee is unhappy about something that happened at work. A better definition: "A grievance is a violation of a specific provision of this agreement that adversely affects the grievant."

WHAT TO AVOID. In addition to overbroad grievance definitions, it is also particularly important to avoid a grievance definition that makes conduct grievable when there are legal remedies available to the employee to remedy the same conduct. For example, Ohio has a statutory procedure for the termination of tenured teaching contracts that includes extensive due process, a hearing, and appeals to court. Any grievance procedure that permitted a grievance based on the termination of that teacher would effectively duplicate the procedures and create an administrative nightmare for management faced with serious misconduct. Similar issues can arise with workplace discrimination claims for which there is an independent state or federal complaint and review process.

The second question involves the grievance procedure itself. Is there, for example, a time limit for the filing of a grievance? What must be included in the formal grievance document, and with whom is it filed? How does the grievance proceed from filing to final resolution? The procedure should have time limits and clearly defined consequences for the failure to timely initiate or advance a grievance to the next level, i.e., grievance over.

Both sides would agree that grievances should be resolved at the lowest level possible. But some grievances involve major issues of contract interpretation and should only be resolved at the highest level of management. The empowerment of a low-level manager to resolve grievances also empowers him or her to make decisions that could have a significant impact on the administration of the contract because the resolution becomes precedent for future grievances. Managers should be cautioned to consult with their supervisors before reaching any agreement to resolve a grievance.

The third and ultimately most significant question is "who makes the final decision?" and the issue is whether the final step is a resolution of the grievance by management or the governing board or by an arbitrator. Many public sector collective bargaining agreements provide for the final resolution of grievances by binding grievance arbitration.[3]

WHAT THE UNION WANTS. The union will argue that arbitration is both faster and cheaper than going to court and provides the benefit of a "neutral" decision by someone familiar with labor-management issues. Management will note, however, that decisions that may carry great financial impact are being made by someone with no accountability to the taxpaying public. Unless required by law, the ultimate decision of whether to include binding grievance arbitration in a contract is made at the bargaining table, and once included, the arbitration provision will probably last as long as the union lasts.

Many agreements that I'm familiar with have provisions for binding grievance arbitration as the final step. If your enterprise is going to agree to grievance arbitration, make sure that management has as much input into the process for the selection of the arbitrator as possible. Many grievances are effectively decided at the point where the arbitrator is selected, simply because they have a "track record" of deciding certain types of grievances either in favor of the union or in favor of management. Be sure to involve your legal counsel in the process at the earliest possible time, and let counsel be involved both in the selection of the arbitrator and the conduct of the arbitration hearing.

While this issue may vary by jurisdiction, it's generally true that arbitration decisions are very difficult to appeal. Both courts and legislatures have expressed a preference for the arbitration process, if agreed to by the parties, and there are often severe limitations on the conditions under which either side can overturn an arbitration decision on appeal. Don't expect to get a bad decision fixed on appeal.

Arbitration can also be costly, and management is often tempted to negotiate a "loser pays" provision into the grievance procedure's arbitration language. While "loser pays" may serve as a deterrent against frivolous grievances, it is also essentially ignored by many arbitrators, some of whom seem to go out of their way to find at least one issue on which to rule in favor of the union in order to avoid one side being the "loser." Splitting the costs between the union and the enterprise is more common, and perhaps more effective.

A sample grievance procedure is found at App. 2.

Transfer, Assignment, and Vacancies

The right to assign and transfer employees and to fill, or not fill, vacancies fits squarely within the definition of management rights. In a perfect management contract, there would be no limitations on that right. But the world isn't perfect, and neither are collective bargaining agreements. Employees want the right to move to better jobs, without limitation by what is often viewed as arbitrary management decisions. So they will often push hard for provisions granting the right to transfer to vacant positions. What follows are some of the considerations that go into the negotiation of those provisions.

Vacancies. The first issue in negotiation of vacancy and transfer provisions is deciding when a vacancy occurs. Sounds simple, right? Maybe not. Issues such as employee absence due to sick leave, maternity leave, disability leave, or other extended leave provisions can cover a whole spectrum of circumstances, and in many cases, the employee has a legal right to return to the same or equivalent position upon return from leave.[4] Suffice to say that in general, if the absent employee has a right to return to the position and is expected to return in a reasonable period of time, the position isn't vacant. Positions that are not vacant should only be filled by temporary substitute employees who acquire no rights to hold the position after the return of the absent employee.

A more difficult question arises when a position is truly vacant because the employee who held the position has left employment and has no right to return. Here, management may wish to either not fill the vacant position at all or to reconfigure the duties. The union wants assurance that each vacant bargaining unit position will be filled with a bargaining unit member, not a temporary employee who may not be included in the bargaining unit. Resolution of this tension may involve a myriad of different possibilities, but in the end, the key issues are: (1) does management have the right to determine whether, and when a vacancy exists; and (2) does management have the assurance that any employee seeking to fill a vacancy is qualified to perform the duties of the job? If the answer is yes to each of those questions, other provisions become far less significant.

TRANSFERS. Transfer and vacancy issues are akin to adjoining rooms in the same hotel. In order to transfer, there must be either a new position within the bargaining unit or a vacant position. As you review the provisions in your contract, here are a couple of things to keep in mind: First, rights to transfer to a different position, if provided at all, should only apply to employees who have a successful track record in the position they currently hold. Transfer should never become an escape hatch for employees who are unable to successfully perform in their current position for at least a minimum period of time. Second, an employee should only have the right to transfer to a vacant position if the employee is fully qualified to perform all of the duties of that position.[5] Third, consider including a trial period for new assignees to the vacant position, permitting the return of that employee to the prior job if performance is not satisfactory.

JOB CLASSIFICATION. Many public sector jobs, especially non-teaching jobs, will fall into "classifications" or categories based on the nature of the primary duties of the position.[6] Bus drivers, for example, may make up one classification; maintenance employees another. Each classification has a unique skill set. While it may well be the case that a school cook could be an excellent school bus driver, it's not necessarily a given that such will be the case. Thus, even if your contract affords employees a right to transfer to vacant positions, it should not afford such a right in the case of cross-classification transfers without some means of assuring that the would-be transferor is in fact qualified to fill the new position.

SENIORITY. Unions generally accept seniority as a fair way to resolve issues that pit one employee against another, such as transfer and layoff. And while seniority is a legitimate consideration, contract provisions that make it the deciding factor in transfer disputes should be drafted carefully. It is not uncommon to find contracts that define two kinds of seniority; the first based on the total time the employee has worked for the enterprise, "system seniority," and the second, "classification seniority" based on the total time the employee has worked in the current job classification. For example, two employees want the same vacant position and the contract provides the job goes to the one with the greatest seniority. One has been employed by the enterprise for fifteen years, with one year as a bus driver (the type of position in question) and fourteen years as a maintenance worker. The other employee has only been employed by the enterprise for ten years, all of which have been spent in the bus driver classification. Which is the more senior? In this instance, the contract language is critical, and far too many contracts overlook this distinction.

Suffice to say that all service is not the same when it comes to seniority for transfer purposes. At the same time, the employee with fifteen years of service to the enterprise has a much stronger argument if the question is which employee should be more senior for layoff purposes.

Many disputes about seniority can be eliminated by a contract provision providing for management to post a seniority list annually, with a period of time for employees to raise any objections to the seniority credited to them on the list. Failure to object would bar any complaints about seniority provided they are credited with the seniority on the list.

A sample contract provision dealing with transfer, assignment, and vacancies is found at App. 3.

Layoff and Recall

Layoff and recall provisions in public sector labor contracts can raise a host of really difficult issues, and the best we can hope for here is a surface review.

What it's about. "Layoff" is a term normally used to describe what happens when an employer has an excess number of employees and needs to reduce the size of the workforce. It is sometimes also called "reduction in force." Regardless of the term used to describe it, layoff results in the workforce becoming smaller, either for a temporary period or a much longer period. On the other side of the coin, "recall" describes the process by which a laid-off employee is recalled to duty by the employer. Unlike termination or voluntary resignation, layoff usually includes recall rights, generally defined as the right to be notified if the employer intends to fill a position in the job classification in which the laid-off employee worked at the time of layoff. It also includes the right to be recalled to the former position rather than it being filled by a new employee. Think of recall rights as a fragile, invisible line connecting the employer and employee after layoff. Instead of ending the employment relationship, layoff suspends it, with the potential for restoration in the event of a recall.

MANAGEMENT INTERESTS. The ability to control the size of the workforce is one of management's most vital interests. If the workforce has become too large, management wants to be able to promptly and predictably reduce its size. At the same time, management also wants to maintain the employees with the necessary skills and experience to continue efficient operations. Any negotiated agreement addressing employee layoff and recall rights should carefully define the recall rights of laid-off employees, including such issues as how long recall rights last, how is notice of recall given, and what are the obligations of the employee to keep management informed of changes in his or her contact information.

UNION INTERESTS. The union wants to avoid, to the extent possible, disputes between employees regarding who should be laid off and who should be retained. Clear contract language benefits everyone in this area. Some unions also want the ability to challenge the employer's decision to lay off bargaining unit employees, either through the grievance procedure or in court.

WHAT TO AVOID. Management wants to avoid limitations on the right to lay off employees when necessary. Management also wants to clearly define the duties of laid-off employees subject to recall. For example, issues including when recall rights expire, does accepting another job while laid off extinguish recall rights, and how quickly must a laid-off employee respond to a recall notice should all be clearly answered.

Recall that earlier we talked about the statutory overlay of laws governing public employment and how those laws interact with various collective bargaining provisions. Layoff and recall issues can highlight some of the difficulties in attempting to comply with rights created by law and rights created by the negotiated agreement.

Here's one example: In many states, public employees have, by law, employment contracts with the enterprise that exist outside of and in addition to the collective bargaining agreement. Teachers, for example, may hold employment contract rights created by law, which may be employment contracts for one or more years ("limited" contracts), or tenure ("continuing" contracts) in their teaching positions. Likewise, many non-teaching employees achieve equivalent job security by reason of legally mandated contracts under state law. [7] If reductions in the size of the workforce are necessary, management must comply with both the statutory rights of its employees and with the rights afforded them in the negotiated agreement. To do this, employers should consider employees who do not have continuing employment status and whose contracts are either expiring or subject to nonrenewal first because ending their employment contracts severs the employment relationship, without recall rights.

For employees under contract not subject to termination or nonrenewal, layoff may be the employer's only option to reduce the size of the workforce. But keep in mind that for those employees, recall rights may well remain.

WHAT TO LOOK FOR. In your contract, there are some key factors that should be covered. First, are the conditions under which management can implement a layoff clearly specified and flexible enough to meet the most likely needs of management? In this regard, the union generally wants to impose very restrictive conditions defining when a layoff can occur, and management wants the unrestricted right to lay off employees whenever it deems it necessary. Many collective bargaining agreements will demonstrate a compromise between these two conflicting positions. As noted above, the conditions of layoff may also be governed by state law. Don't hesitate to consult with your legal counsel if necessary to get a full understanding of how your contract should address these issues.

Second, how is a layoff determined? The second and most difficult step is determining *who* is to be laid off. This may look easy at first, but often it is not. For example, let's assume that a job is abolished because those particular duties are no longer needed. The person in that job is the most likely target for layoff. But wait, in your contract, layoff is determined by seniority, and the person in that job is not the least senior employee in that job classification. Enter the concept of "bumping," a provision in which a senior employee targeted for layoff can replace a less senior employee through the exercise of contract rights. The "bumped" employee is the one actually losing his or her job. All of this suggests that the contract should address the questions of how seniority is accrued and exercised in a manner that avoids uncertainty. Most layoff issues never arise until an actual layoff becomes necessary, and at that point, employees will do whatever is necessary to keep their jobs. The best approach is to resolve uncertainties before they become life-or-death issues for the employees, and your contract is the best place to do that.

HOW LONG CAN I BE LAID OFF? I've seen recall rights lasting from a number of months to three years. At some point, an employee who has not been recalled should no longer have the right to be recalled. One of the most common, and most serious, mistakes management makes is to assume that an employee who has not been recalled is no longer an employee. If the contract provides for "callback" rights, which usually occur when a job opening occurs in the classification from which the employee was laid off, the employee may have had a right to be recalled, regardless of whether he or she has taken another job in the meantime. Management's failure to offer recall to that employee can create a liability that could easily have been avoided. Make sure that your contract specifies how long callback rights exist, how notifications take place, and what happens at the end of the callback period.

A sample layoff provision is included at App. 4.

EMPLOYEE DISCIPLINE AND DISCHARGE

Absent a collective bargaining agreement, the rights of public employees to tenure in any position will vary from state to state. Public employees, due to the nature of the employer, will often have more job security than employees in the private sector, primarily as a vestige of the pre-collective bargaining days when public sector jobs were generally afforded lower pay and benefits than their private sector counterparts. State civil service laws affording statutory tenure rights are not uncommon as examples of pre-collective bargaining structures used to create job security for many public employees. With the advent of public sector collective bargaining, discipline and discharge provisions have become common in public sector contracts, and an understanding of what they mean and how they work is critical to effective bargaining.

Management's bargaining position on employee discipline issues is tempered by the fact that, unlike their private-sector counterparts, many public employment positions have been recognized as a "property right" of the individual employee that cannot be diminished or extinguished for disciplinary reasons without the employee first having been afforded due process of law.[8] In this context, due process essentially means that before an employee can be terminated, he or she is, at a minimum, entitled to notice of the alleged violation and an opportunity to explain. But beyond that minimum, circumstances can vary widely, and I've had statutory teacher termination hearings that lasted for weeks and resembled full-blown trials. What's important here is to recognize that when discipline involves potential termination or a reduction in pay or position, some sort of due process may be required before any discipline can be imposed.

Employee discipline is the imposition of an adverse consequence for workplace behavior that is prohibited. The consequence can fall in a spectrum ranging from a verbal warning e.g. "you screwed up, don't do it again," to a written warning, a formal reprimand, suspension without pay, reassignment to a lesser position, or even termination. Managers are usually empowered to impose discipline within statutory and contractual guidelines. However, in jurisdictions where the governing board of the public body is also the "hiring official" it generally falls to the governing board to impose the ultimate discipline—termination.

A word of caution about informal discipline. Most employee discipline is cumulative—that is, rather than a single act, employee discipline and the appropriate level of consequences escalates based not only on the current conduct giving rise to discipline, but also the prior conduct of the employee. In that context, "informal discipline" is still discipline, and notes of the conduct as well as the consequences should become part of the personnel file for consideration in the event that future discipline should become warranted. The same concerns argue against union proposals for "file cleansing," or the removal of references to discipline after a period of time.

Volumes have been written attempting to describe "cause," "good cause," or "just cause" in the context of employee discipline. Here, suffice to say that discipline should be limited to the job-related conduct in violation of established work rules.

Here's an example: Suppose that a governing board member observed a schoolteacher in the local bar having a beer one evening. The board member, believing that the teacher's presence in the bar reflected adversely on the public image of the school, proposed to discipline the teacher for that conduct, even though there were no written rules or other specific prohibitions in place. In that circumstance, the discipline would likely fail because the conduct being disciplined is sufficiently remote from the teacher's duties. Compare that with the teacher showing up for work under the influence of alcohol. In that instance, there is a direct relationship between the conduct and the teacher's job assignment, and discipline would be appropriate.

Unions want the collective bargaining agreement to define the specific types of conduct that will be subject to discipline, while employers want to retain the essential management rights to define and change work rules as needed, and to discipline employees who fail to follow those rules without having to deal with contractual limitations. Most mature public sector contracts attempt to compromise between these two extremes.

Termination of employment is the ultimate penalty, and depending on the nature of the position, potential career death for the employee as well. In cases involving termination there is no question that due process is required, either by state or federal law. But what you don't want is to create contractual procedures that disagree or perhaps conflict with any applicable statutory requirements. Thus, where there are extensive termination procedures prescribed by state law, your contract should commit to nothing more than to "follow the law" with respect to termination procedures.

The same is true for disciplinary grievances. Unions will want, to the fullest extent possible, to be able to challenge discipline and termination actions by way of grievance. At the same time, employers will argue that the statutory termination procedure is sufficient due process and that the employee shouldn't get two bites at the apple. Negotiators should be aware of the "two-forum" issue and craft language to ensure that the employee only gets one bite.

State and federal laws provide a wide range of protections for employees who believe they have been wrongfully terminated or denied other benefits of employment because of a lawfully protected status or conduct. For example, federal law prohibits discrimination based on a wide range of characteristics, including sex, race, national origin, and in some cases age, among others.[9] Those laws also provide for legal remedies that can include both reinstatement and back pay and in some cases, money damages and attorney fees.[10] Regardless of the rules in your state, most of the federal employment protection laws exist beyond the range of collective bargaining, and you simply can't, by contract, prevent a terminated employee from seeking any of these remedies. What you can do, however, is to provide for the termination of any grievance brought by the terminated employee in the event that the same circumstances become the subject of a formal complaint in another forum.

WHAT THE UNION WANTS. The union wants to avoid arbitrary discipline of employees and to limit the ability of management to impose arbitrary or unreasonable discipline to the extent possible. In that regard, having the ability to challenge discipline through the grievance procedure often becomes an issue.

WHAT MANAGEMENT WANTS. The right to discipline employees for job-related misconduct is generally considered one of the essential rights of management. Accordingly, management will tend to resist provisions that would encroach on the exercise of those rights. At the same time, neither side has an interest in promoting arbitrary disciplinary decisions. The adage, "The best contract won't make up for bad management, and the worst contract won't diminish good management" is often appropriate in the area of employee discipline. That said, clearly defined contract rights and responsibilities are, nonetheless, very important.

A sample Discipline and Discharge provision is included at App. 5.

LEAVES

For our discussion here, a "leave" means an excused absence from work, which can occur either with or without pay. The right to leave can arise from legislation, such as the Family and Medical Leave Act, or from the contract. Many contracts contain a virtual laundry list of leaves, such as vacation leave, sick leave, disability leave, maternity leave, bereavement leave, etc. Rather than reviewing each potential type of leave or discussion, here we will deal with management considerations in the grant and administration of leave provisions generally.

WHAT THE UNION WANTS. As a general matter, the union tends to view leave provisions, especially paid leaves, as employee rights and will resist limitations on the accrual and use of those rights. On the other hand, management views paid leave provisions as costs. Paid leave entails payment of compensation for time when no work is performed, and often the payment of a substitute employee as well. Leave provisions can also jeopardize the ability to maintain operations. If all or a vital segment of employees were absent on leave at the same time, the employer might be unable to maintain operations.

The first question related to any leave provision is how the right to leave arises. The right to leave can exist because of state law, federal law, or the collective bargaining agreement. Family and Medical Leave, for example, exists because of federal law and creates a minimum level of benefits.[11] In Ohio, sick leave for regular public schoolteachers accrues by state law at the rate of fifteen days per year.[12] Other types of leave can arise solely because of the collective bargaining agreement.

For example, in some Ohio school districts, the first day of deer hunting season is always an unpaid leave day because school is closed that day, by contract. Individual leave entitlements should specify exactly how and when the entitlement accrues. For example, if an employee is entitled to two weeks' vacation leave per year, exactly when does that entitlement accrue? In some cases, it might accrue on the anniversary of employment, or in others, it might accrue incrementally, with a portion of the vacation leave credited every month. Failure to specify accrual can lead to numerous disputes.

In some cases, contract provisions will permit accrued and unused leaves, especially sick leave, to be paid in whole or in part as an additional benefit upon the retirement of the employee ("Severance Pay"). Severance pay provisions can become a large financial obligation for the enterprise, and care should be taken when negotiating such provisions in a contract. In one especially badly drafted example, an enterprise was forced to make a large severance payment to an employee whom it fired for malfeasance simply because the payment was due on the severance of employment rather than retirement from employment.

Another issue to look for in reviewing leave provisions relates to when and how the leave may be used. Here, the question is whether the employer is entitled to receive advance notice of the intended absence. Vacations, elective surgery, and even pregnancy leave can be known well in advance of the intended absence, and the employee should provide as much advance notice as possible. In some cases the use of leaves may be limited to specific times of the year, or conditioned on the availability of a substitute, if necessary.[13]

The most commonly abused leave provision in the public sector is sick leave, and employees who create a pattern of "calling off sick" on Fridays or Mondays, especially in the spring, are particularly suspect. But if challenged, the denial of sick leave places the burden on the employer, and proving that someone is "not sick" on a given day can be a challenge. Here's a case in point: A teacher who had called in sick was spotted at a golf tournament by the board president. The teacher's sick leave request was denied, and he filed a grievance that ultimately went to arbitration. Admitting that he had been at the golf tournament, he testified that he had been too sick to come to work in the morning, but got better and went to the tournament because it was too late in the day to go to school. The arbitrator bought that story, and the teacher got his sick leave.

One of the most common ways to verify illness is a doctor's note, attesting to the fact that the employee was unable to report to work on a given day. Unions generally oppose a doctor-note requirement for verification of minor illness. However, if management can demonstrate patterns of sick leave usage suggesting that abuse is actually happening, it is much easier to put verification requirements into the contract.

Long-term leaves that don't have a specified ending date can be difficult to manage, and periodic updates on the status of the employee are helpful. Whatever the reason for the leave, a long-term absence generally means that the vacant position cannot be filled with a permanent employee. In this circumstance, it's a good idea to require advance notice of intent to return or, if the employee decides not to return, notice of that as well.

WHAT MANAGEMENT WANTS. As the foregoing indicates, some types of leave can exist because of employee statutory rights while others exist because the negotiated agreement provides for them. Regardless of the source, management's primary concern is maintaining the ability to operate the enterprise. That often means, first, that it has as much advance notice of intended absence from duty as possible, and second, that it has the ability to fill the vacancy caused by the leave with a qualified employee. In the case of a long-term leave, the employer also needs as much advance notice of the employee's intent to return as possible, and the ability to assign or reassign work duties to accommodate the return of the absent employee. Additionally, the ability to verify the reasons for the leave becomes important when circumstances suggest a potential pattern of abuse.

A sample leave provision is included at App. 6.

UNION DUES

Dues are the financial lifeblood of the union and have tradition-ally been paid by employer deductions from the payroll of bar-gaining unit employees, whether they have chosen to join the union or not. Thus, while union members agreed to the deduc-tion of union dues, those who chose not to join the union were, nonetheless, required to pay the equivalent of union dues through "agency fee" payroll deductions. In many states, laws had been passed to permit the deduction of agency fees and that practice had been upheld by the United States Supreme Court.[14]

All of that was changed by the United States Supreme Court's decision in *Janus v. American Federation of State, County, and Municipal Employees, Council 31, ET Al.*[15] *Janus* is important for a number of reasons. First, the decision struck down the use of "agency fee" provisions that required non-union bargaining unit members to pay for the support of union activities related to collective bargaining in lieu of union dues. Second, the decision leaves the door open for other workplace challenges by those who, like the plaintiff in *Janus*, believe that employer workplace rules violate their First Amendment rights.

Some background is necessary to understand the issues involved in the *Janus* decision. As noted earlier, the concept of "collective" bargaining envelops individual employee concerns into a single "union" focus. Thus, when collective bargaining is required, the employer must deal with the union, not the individual employees, on workplace issues. In the public sector, this model is usually based on state legislation describing a process by which a union is selected as the exclusive bargaining representative of a specific bargaining unit of employees. The union so selected acquires a franchise as the "exclusive bargaining representative" for those employees. Along with that status, the union also generally acquires an obligation to represent all employees in the bargaining unit, whether or not they join the union and pay union dues. Since union membership is not mandatory, this creates a circumstance by which employees can choose not to join and refuse to pay union dues, thus enjoying the benefits of bargaining and representation without any obligation to pay for those benefits. Often these folks are described as "free riders."

Illinois, as well as numerous other states, had enacted legislation permitting public sector collective bargaining agreements to include agency fee provisions. The Supreme Court had expressly upheld public sector agency fee payments over forty years earlier in *Abood v. Detroit Bd. Of Ed.*, 431 U.S. 209 (1977). *Abood* held that the collection of agency fees was permissible, so long as the fees excluded amounts used by the union for political causes. Thus, while the Supreme Court in *Abood* recognized the free speech implications of mandatory union support, it also recognized that effective bargaining entails expenses that are properly assigned to those employees who enjoy the benefits of bargaining. Since the public employers also benefit from collective bargaining, they have a legitimate interest in the agency fee provisions that justifies their making the involuntary wage deductions from the payrolls of non-union employees. That interest, the court determined, was sufficient to justify the use of agency fees.

The *Janus* decision highlights one of the most significant distinctions between public and private sector bargaining in that actions by a public employer constitute "state action" regardless of whether directed to members of the public or the governmental agency's employees and must not infringe on the constitutional rights of either.[16] Thus, while a private-sector employer can make workplace rules that limit the First Amendment rights of employees in the workplace, public employers are subject to a much higher level of scrutiny regarding the same sort of restrictions.[17] That's not to say that public employers are unable to regulate the speech of their employees; rather, they may do so only when the regulations serve the public interest and are narrowly tailored to impose the least practicable limitation on employee rights. It was against this background that the *Janus* case came to the Supreme Court.

The plaintiff in *Janus* was an employee of the State of Illinois who asserted that the forced payment of agency fees to the union representing state employees, a union that he had refused to join, violated his First Amendment rights by forcing him to support union positions with which he disagreed. The Supreme Court agreed in a five-to-four decision led by the conservative majority of the court in a lengthy opinion written by Justice Alito followed by a strong dissent from Justice Kagan.

Both sides agreed that the fundamental legal issue in the case, the payment of agency fees, implicated the First Amendment rights of public employees, including Janus. Here, the "speech" being challenged was not active speech but the right not to speak through whatever support the forced payment of agency fees gave to the union. However, the underlying agency fee issue went far beyond Mr. Janus's unspecified objections to agency fee payments and dealt with the extent of union empowerment in the public sector generally.

The only way the court could rule in favor of the plaintiff was to reverse its prior decision in *Abood*. Seeking to justify that reversal, Justice Alito, writing for the majority of the court, found that *Abood* had been wrongly decided in the first instance. According to Justice Alito, neither of the primary circumstances relied on by the court in *Abood* warranted the justification of agency fees. First, the argument that agency fees promoted a public-sector management interest in labor peace was rejected, relying primarily on both federal and state examples in which unions apparently functioned without the benefit of agency fee collection.

The second argument justifying agency fees in *Abood*, that agency fees were necessary to prevent "free riders," was also dispatched by Justice Alito, noting "…[i]t is simply not true that unions will refuse to serve as the exclusive representative of all employees in the unit if they are not given agency fees. No union is ever compelled to seek that designation." Id at 14.

Having concluded that *Abood* was wrongly decided in the first instance and that there were no other legitimate reasons for upholding it, the court proceeded to overrule it. The court's conclusion stated, "… States and public-sector unions may no longer extract agency fees from nonconsenting employees. *** Neither an agency fee nor any other payment to the union may be deducted from a nonmember's wages, nor may any other attempt be made to collect such a payment, unless the employee affirmatively consents to pay." Id at 48.

As a consequence, public-sector unions can no longer collect fees or dues from non-members simply because it has negotiated an agency fee provision into the collective bargaining agreement. While agency fee provisions can still be found in some contracts, they are no longer enforceable. However, predictions of dire consequences for public-sector unions as the result of the *Janus* decision have, for the most part, failed to materialize. If anything, the decision has forced unions to work harder to prove their worth to the members of the bargaining units they represent. Employers can continue to deduct union dues from the wages of union members, provided the members consent to those deductions.[18]

A potential problem for both public-sector unions and employers is the continuing obligation of union to fairly represent all bargaining unit members, whether they pay dues or not. If the union is not as vigilant in representing a non-dues-paying bargaining unit member, it could be charged with an unfair labor practice. The public employer must be cautious not to appear to collude with the union if there appears to be a failure to advocate for the member and the employee is left to represent his or her own interests without union assistance.

Additionally, *Janus* left the door open for unions to charge non-union-dues-paying members for representational services. This may present a bargaining challenge for public employers as there is no reason for them to negotiate such a provision into the contract. There are a few contracts, however, that have been negotiated, post-*Janus,* where an employer has agreed that the union may charge reasonable costs for services, to the extent allowed by law.

"Before and after" agency fee and union dues deduction provisions are included at App. 7.

WHAT TO LOOK FOR. As you review your contract keep in mind that crucial changes have taken place, removing the legal authority of the employer to deduct union dues from the wages of non-union employees. If your contract continues to provide for these deductions, it should be changed. Likewise, if your enterprise continues to deduct union dues (agency fees) from the wages of non-union employees you should consult with your legal counsel about changing this practice as soon as possible. Make sure that any new provisions comply with the *Janus* requirements.

NEGOTIATIONS

Most public sector collective bargaining agreements have ending dates. In Ohio, for example, the maximum duration is three years, and those dates serve as the trigger for the bargaining of a new, successor agreement. In Part I, we reviewed the processes by which that bargaining is accomplished, but the "negotiations" provisions in most agreements provide, at most, a bare-bones structure. Here are some of the more common items you are likely to see in your contract:

TIMING. Negotiations are usually set to begin well before the end of the existing contract, usually somewhere between 120 and 60 days prior to the ending date.

SUBMISSION OF PROPOSALS. It is also not uncommon to see provisions requiring both sides to submit all bargaining proposals at the initial meeting unless agreed otherwise. As noted earlier, this is an expectation, whether expressly stated or not.

BARGAINING TEAMS. The size and composition of bargaining teams for each side is often described in the negotiations provision, as well as provisions for changes in team membership, observers, and invited participants for specific issues. Other than authorized participants, bargaining meetings are usually closed to the public.

IMPASSE. It is also not uncommon to see negotiations provisions address the process to be followed upon impasse. As noted in Part

I, the procedures for the resolution of impasse can have a substantial impact on the bargaining strategies followed by the parties.

Regardless of the contracted procedures, keep in mind that the parties to the bargaining process, union, and management, are always free to change or modify those procedures, so long as both sides agree to the change.

WHAT MANAGEMENT WANTS. I believe that both sides benefit from using the IBB approach to bargaining, and inclusion of that process in the negotiations provision will serve to solidify that commitment. Additionally, a pre-bargaining meeting for the exchange of proposals will help focus the areas of preparation needed for effective bargaining. Management also wants to have the right individuals at the bargaining table to address the issues being discussed at the time, and this may require the ability to either add to or substitute members of its bargaining team as circumstances require. Management may also want to ensure that information exchanged before actual bargaining begins is covered by the confidentiality provisions of the agreement, if any.

WHAT THE UNION WANTS. The more traditional union bargainers will seek to have the longest possible period for bargaining the successor contract and a look at management's proposals at the earliest possible time. Union bargaining team members will want to be "on the clock" during bargaining and will ask management to foot-the-bill for any bargaining expenses. As with all other bargaining issues, these items are negotiable.

A sample negotiations provision is included at App. 8.

ROLLOVER OF UNCHANGED CONTRACT LANGUAGE

Though seldom found as a stand-alone provision, most contracts will contain, somewhere, language that essentially states that any provision in the existing contract that was not expressly amended or deleted during the negotiations for a successor agreement will be carried forward into the new agreement. Though seemingly innocuous, such a provision essentially means that any provision put into a collective bargaining agreement will remain part of that agreement until both sides agree to change or remove it. Of course, this can be changed, and I've often negotiated "sunset" language attached to specific contract provisions that we didn't want in the contract forever. But, absent something like that, be aware that once a provision is placed in the contract it tends to stay there for a very long time.

Sample rollover language can be found in App. 8 Article V(C).

Preface

The following are contract provisions that provide examples of issues we reviewed in Part II. As you consider these provisions, keep in mind that they are not offered as examples of "best practice." Rather, they are offered to demonstrate the end result of bargaining that may have taken place over multiple contract negotiations. You will see provisions that favor management and provisions that favor the union, all of which demonstrate the nature of compromises made at the bargaining table. In selecting these provisions I've drawn from three different types of bargaining units: municipal, public school teaching, and public school non-teaching. Of course, there are many other types of public sector bargaining units, but you will likely see the same types of provisions in their contracts as well. There are many other types of issues normally found in public sector agreements, such as union rights, insurance, payroll, local work rules, and other local provisions far too numerous to mention. But the goal here is not to make you an expert on every possible negotiation issue. Rather, the goal is to give you a sound understanding of the process so that you can effectively deal with any issue brought forward for negotiations, regardless of how unique it might be. I believe the contract provisions included below contribute to that end.

RECOGNITION

A. The Board recognizes _____
Educational Support Staff Association/OEA/NEA, hereinafter referred to as the Association, as the sole and exclusive bargaining representative for all full-time regular and regular short-hour (10 or more hours per week) employees in the following classifications: Secretary 1, 2, and 3; Clerk Typist 1 and 2; Accountant 1, 2, and 3; Health Aide; Study Hall/Building Duty Monitor; ESL Paraprofessional Bilingual Aide; ESL Paraprofessional; and Instructional Technologists/Technology Clerk. Employees excluded from the bargaining unit are those employed in the following classifications or positions: Supervisors; Administrative Grade Secretaries 1, 2, and 3; Insurance and Benefits Secretary; Secretary 2 to the Assistant Superintendent; Accountant 2 for Payroll (Classified Employees); Accountant 2 for Payroll (Certificated Employees); Customer Service Representatives at the Welcome Center; as needed interpreters/ translators; substitutes, short-hour (less than 10 hours per week), and any and all other positions in the school district.

B. For the purpose of determining full-time employment for the unit, the following schedule* shall be used.

12-month employee (typically contracted for 260 days/year) 1,950 hours per year

11-month employee (typically contracted for 239 days/year) 1,792.5 hours per year

10-month employee (typically contracted for 215 days/year) 1,612.5 hours per year

9-month employee (typically contracted for 195 days/year) 1,462.5 hours per year

*The calculation for this schedule shall be 7.5 hours per day times the number of contracted days, which includes paid holidays.

In the event the number of annual contracted days for a category of employees (e.g., 10-month employees), which includes paid holidays, decreases then the calculations above shall be adjusted accordingly so as not to adversely impact any member in that category of employees.

C. The Board and the Association agree that the Board may from time to time hire "supplemental help." The term "supplemental help" shall mean the contracting of outside sources to perform work for the duration of one (1) to sixty (60) calendar days in a secretary/health aide/clerk/accounting position that did not previously exist. It is not the intent of this section to interfere with the practice of hiring "supplemental help." After the sixty (60) day time period, the District shall fill the position in accordance with the procedures under Article X, following approval by the Board through the Board's appropriation of All Funds, if it is determined by the Superintendent that the position is needed on an ongoing basis. If not, the _____, president shall be notified that the position is not to be filled at that time and the supplemental help will cease at the end of the sixty (60) day time period. The Board shall not purposely terminate the employment of a person in such a position before the sixty (60) calendar days, and then fill the same position with the same person or another person for the purposes of avoiding these provisions. The Board agrees to keep the _____ President apprised of any such "supplemental help" work performed in the District.

AUTHOR'S NOTE:

RECOGNITION. As noted in the text, the primary purpose of the recognition clause is: (1) to recognize the union as the bargaining representative of a group of employees, and (2) to define those positions that are in, and not in, that group. This provision accomplishes that purpose.

Grievance Process

SECTION 1.

It is mutually understood that the prompt presentation, adjustment, and/or resolution of grievances is desirable in the interest of sound relations between bargaining unit employees and the City.

SECTION 2.

The term "grievance" shall mean an allegation by a bargaining unit employee and/or the Union that there has been a breach, misinterpretation, or improper application of this Agreement. Newly hired probationary employees shall not be permitted access to this grievance procedure for any disciplinary, layoff, or discharge action taken by the City during their probationary period. The parties agree that it is their mutual desire to provide for the prompt adjustment of grievances with a minimum amount of disruption to work schedules. Every reasonable effort will be made by the parties to effect the resolution of grievances at the earliest step possible. Accordingly, grievances shall be processed in the following manner:

STEP 1: The employee and the employee's Division manager shall meet to discuss and attempt to resolve the grievance on an informal basis. However, if the grievance is not resolved through the informal method, the Union may file a written grievance with his or her immediate supervisor within ten (10) workdays as defined in Section 6. Within two (2) work days after the filing of the written grievance, the appropriate management representatives, the aggrieved employee(s), and, a representative of the Union shall meet to discuss the matter. Within seven (7) workdays after this meeting, the appropriate management representative shall issue a written response to the grievance.

STEP 2: If the grievance is not resolved in Step 1, the Union may appeal in writing the Step 1 response to the Department Director or his or her designee within seven (7) workdays after receipt of the Step 1 response. The Department Director or designee shall schedule a grievance meeting with the aggrieved employee(s) and a representative of the Union, within seven (7) workdays after receipt of the appeal. The Department Director or designee shall issue a written decision to the grievance within seven (7) workdays after this grievance meeting.

STEP 3: If the grievance is not resolved in Step 2, the Union may file an appeal in writing to the City Manager, or with his/her designated representative, within seven (7) workdays after receipt of the Step 2 decision. The City Manager or designated representative shall reply in writing within ten (10) workdays thereafter.

SECTION 3.

A group grievance may be brought at Step 2 of the grievance process and filed within seven (7) workdays as defined in Section 6. A group grievance is defined as one which immediately and adversely affects all or a substantial group of bargaining unit employees, in addition to the employee filing the grievance.

SECTION 4.

Written grievances must contain the following information:

1. Date and time that the incident giving rise to the grievance occurred;
2. General narrative description of the incident giving rise to grievance;
3. Specific provisions of this Agreement alleged to have been violated or misapplied;
4. Specific relief requested;
5. Printed name and signature of the employee; and
6. Name of the aggrieved employee's supervisor and the date on which the grievance was informally discussed with that supervisor.

SECTION 5. ARBITRATION PROCEDURE.

(A) If the grievance remains unresolved following the decision of the City Manager, the Union may submit said grievance to arbitration under the rules of the Federal Mediation and Conciliation Service or another mutually agreed third party. Such action shall be taken within thirty (30) calendar days following the decision of the City Manager. If FMCS is chosen, the panel shall be from the National Academy Panel where possible. Either party may request a second panel from FMCS. If the Union fails to submit said grievance to arbitration, the grievance shall be deemed abandoned and no further action shall be taken with respect to such grievance.

(B) The Arbitrator shall convene a hearing at the earliest possible date for the purpose of hearing the grievance.

1. The Arbitrator shall have no authority to amend, modify, nullify, add to, or subtract from the specific written provisions of this Agreement. The Arbitrator shall only consider and make a decision with respect to the specific issue in dispute and shall have no authority to make a decision on any other issue. The Arbitrator shall provide the parties with a decision within thirty (30) days following the close of the hearing. The Arbitrator's decision shall be final and binding on all parties as to the matter in dispute.

2. Nothing in this section shall limit the right of the parties to be represented by legal counsel during the arbitration process.

3. The fees and expenses of the Arbitrator will be shared equally by each party. All other expenses shall be borne by the party incurring them. Neither party shall be responsible for any of the expenses incurred by the other party. The City will provide a hearing room for any hearings or meetings related to the arbitration process.

4. If either party desires a transcript of the proceedings, it may cause a transcript to be recorded; provided that the party that arranges to have the transcript recorded shall be the party that pays all fees associated with such transcript. Copies of any

transcripts recorded or generated during the arbitration process shall be made available to the other party within a reasonable time after a request is made therefor.

5. Any solution or award recommended by the Arbitrator may be retroactive to the date on which the event giving rise to the grievance occurred, or up to five (5) days prior to that time, if the event occurred within that time period. In no event shall a grievance be deemed to have occurred prior to the effective date of this Agreement, except as specifically acknowledged and identified in writing by the parties on the date this Agreement is signed.

SECTION 6. TIME LIMITATIONS.

A grievance must be filed within ten (10) workdays from the occurrence of the event that gives rise to the grievance, or within ten (10) workdays of the time at which there is reasonable knowledge of such event. If an employee or the Union has taken timely action with respect to any step in the grievance process and the City fails to respond in a timely manner, the employee or the Union, as appropriate, shall be entitled to advance the grievance to the next step in the grievance process, but shall not be required to do so.

(A) Should the Union fail to take the action necessary to file a grievance or advance a grievance to the next step in the grievance process under the time frames set forth herein, the matter shall be considered resolved, and the employee, and the Union on that employee's behalf, shall be barred from grieving the same issue in connection with the same event or circumstance.

(B) The parties may, by mutual agreement, extend the time frames for responding to or filing any item required as part of the grievance process established above.

SECTION 7.

The Union shall have final authority, in its capacity as exclusive representative of the employees covered by this Agreement, to withdraw or terminate the processing of a grievance at any step of the established grievance process.

SECTION 8.

The grievance process established in this Article shall be the sole and exclusive method for resolving grievances under this Agreement. Any decisions, results, or settlements reached under the terms of this grievance process shall be final, conclusive, and binding on the City, the Union, and the bargaining unit employees.

AUTHOR'S NOTE:

GRIEVANCE PROCEDURE. This provision contains elements common to many grievance procedures in use today. Note that binding arbitration is the final step.

Transfer, Assignment, and Vacancies

Bidding Procedures and Lateral Transfers

VACANCIES

5.1 When new permanent positions become available or permanent vacancies occur, employees and the Local President will be notified in writing regarding the vacancy. Employees must reply in writing within five (5) working days after the date of the written memorandum regarding the vacancy. Vacancies which exist because of the creation of a new position shall always be subject to posting and bidding procedures before implementation of lateral or involuntary transfer procedures.

Vacancies shall be posted by _____ building representatives for five (5) working days in each building staffed by employees of the bargaining unit. Such notices shall be posted in designated open areas accessible to all employees in each building.

Employees desiring a vacant position shall submit their bid in writing to the designated administrator within the five (5) working day posting period. The "vacancy notice" shall contain a job title, qualifications that may include but shall not be limited to the job description, shift, work location(s), and the deadline (hour and day) for submitting a bid.

5.2 The vacancy shall be awarded to the applicant with the greatest class seniority. In the event two (2) or more employees within the same class series bid on the same job, the one with the greatest class series seniority will be awarded the position. Employees bidding on a vacant position who are not within the class series will be considered for the vacant position: (1) first on level of qualifications (including test scores. A minimum passing score shall be established and communicated to the employee prior to taking the test.) (2) if two or more employees in the same classification which encompasses the class series in which the vacancy exists are equally qualified, the position will be awarded the employee with greatest classification seniority in that classification; (3) if two or more employees are equally qualified and none has classification seniority, then the position will be awarded the employee with the greatest district seniority. The Board shall be the sole judge of qualifications. Bidding shall be permitted only for the original permanent vacancy. Any other vacancy shall be filled through lateral transfer procedures. The Board has the right to establish minimum qualifications for each vacancy to be filled and may require the passage of a test as a condition of employee transfer to a different class series or classification.

5.3 After the five (5) working day posting period, and dependent upon the internal transfer, vacancies shall be filled within twenty (20) working days of receipt of test results.

5.4 Any newly created or vacant bus route shall be awarded to the most senior driver who bids on the position. The route vacated by the successful bidder shall be offered to the most senior driver who bids on the original route. If all individuals who bid on the original vacancy refuse this position, it shall be given to a substitute, and there shall be no further bidding only after the original bid list has been exhausted.

5.5 The Superintendent or his/her designee and the employee shall each have a ninety (90) working day trial period within which to determine the fitness, adaptability, and suitability of the employee to the new assignment. Days spent on leave will not count towards completion of an employee's probation period. If either party determines that the employee does not meet these criteria for the new job and so notifies the other party in writing within the ninety (90) working day period, the employee shall be reassigned to his/her former position.

LATERAL TRANSFER PROCEDURES

5.6 Each school year in the month of May the administration will provide employees an opportunity to place their name on a transfer list for a change of job assignment for which the unit member is qualified within the same class series. In addition, each October there will be a supplemental sign-up period in which the employees may add positions to their transfer list, not to exceed the limit contained in Section 5.7. This procedure does not apply to a change in job classifications. The Superintendent or his/her designee will maintain a master transfer list for those individuals desiring a change of job assignments, a copy of said list will, upon request, be provided to the Association President by June 15th, or November 15th, as applicable. Procedures and time limits for the completion of transfer forms will be posted in each building in the same manner as the posting of vacancies. Transfer forms may be obtained from the personnel office and will also be available in each building.

5.7 Employees may list assignment, shift, location, and hours in order of preference up to three (3) choices.

5.8 When a second vacancy results due to District's bidding procedure, those employees desiring a transfer will be considered for the position on the basis of class series seniority. Employees who have indicated a desire to transfer will be notified of a vacant position and will have until the end of the workday following the workday on which they were notified to indicate whether they are willing to accept the transfer. Employees who are notified of a vacancy at times other than during a regularly scheduled workday will have a minimum of twenty-four (24) hours in which to indicate whether they are willing to accept the transfer. Any employee who would have been transferred had he or she accepted the transfer within the response period and who fails to respond to the notice within the response period, or who responds that he or she does not desire to be transferred, will be considered as having refused the lateral transfer. Whenever possible, notice will indicate whether one or more employees with greater seniority have also indicated a desire to make a lateral transfer to the same position.

5.9 Those employees who were eligible to be transferred but refused to accept the transfer will have their names removed from the list and may not reapply until the next period begins (May or October).

5.10 No employee who is given a transfer may have his/her name placed on the transfer list again for a period of one (1) year.

5.11 After the transfer procedures have been completed, remaining vacancies shall be filled by the Superintendent.

5.12 The Superintendent or his/her designee and the employees shall each have a ninety (90) working day trial period within which to determine the fitness, adaptability, and suitability of the employee to the new assignment. Days spent on leave will not count towards completion of an employee's probation period. If either party determines that the employee does not meet these criteria for the new job and so notifies the other party in writing within the ninety (90) working day period, the employee shall be reassigned to his/her former position.

5.13 In order to meet the staffing needs of the District, it may be necessary to reassign a classified employee involuntarily. Prior to such action, representatives from the Administration and the Association shall meet to discuss the staffing needs causing the involuntary transfer. Such transfer shall be made after consultation with the appropriate supervisor and the classified employee affected by the transfer. In no case shall an employee be transferred without first having been involved in a conference explaining the need for such transfer. Unless proven to be arbitrary or capricious, administrative decisions on all such transfers are final.

AUTHOR'S NOTE:

TRANSFER, ASSIGNMENT, AND VACANCIES. Although the title of this provision differs from the title discussed in the text, the subject matter is the same. Transfer and assignment provisions can be as complex as the composition of the bargaining unit, but the goals remain the same. For the enterprise, assurance of a qualified employee to fill a vacant position, and for the union, assurance of a fair opportunity for advancement to a better position when one becomes available.

Layoff and Recall

1.3 LAYOFF AND RECALL PROCEDURE

A. If the Board determines it is necessary to reduce the number of permanent employees in a job classification because of abolishment of positions, lack of funds, or lack of work, the following procedures shall govern such layoff in lieu of the procedures in Section 124.321 - 124.328 of the Ohio Revised Code and Rule X111 of the _____ Civil Service Rules. Substitute, seasonal, and casual employees may be laid off for the reasons set forth above but are not subject to the provisions below.

B. The number of employees affected by reduction in force will be kept to a minimum by not employing replacements in so far as practical for employees who resign, retire, or otherwise vacate a position.

C. Whenever it is necessary to lay off employees for reasons set forth above, the following order of preference shall be followed within each classification: a) full- and part-time provisional employees shall be laid off first; b) full- and part-time proba-tionary employees shall be laid off next; c) part-time permanent (fewer than six (6) hours per day) employees shall be laid off next; d) full-time permanent employees (six (6) hours per day or more) shall be laid off next. Within each classification or classification series, employees shall be laid off in the order of seniority in the affected classification with the least senior employee within the classification or classification series laid off first. Seniority shall be calculated from the most recent date of hire in the current job classification series. A seniority list will be submitted to the WESP president by February 15 of each year. Any challenge to the stated seniority must be presented in writing not later than ten (10) working days after submission of the seniority list. All unchallenged seniority shall be deemed valid for all purposes. If two or more employees have identical seniority, the tie shall be broken by lot. Approved leaves of absence shall not be consid-ered a break in service. Approved unpaid leaves of absence greater than ten (10) cumulative workdays per calendar year shall not be counted toward seniority. Employees who have been absent by reason of a work-related injury for which workers' compen-sation benefits have been awarded and paid may, upon return to duty, be credited with seniority for the time of absence. Any employee desiring seniority credit for work-related injury absence must request such credit by written application to the Human Resources Department. For purposes of this section, a calendar year begins on August 1 and ends on July 31.

D. The job classifications to be used in the event of a layoff are those set forth in Section 5.3(f). The Board shall determine in which classification any layoff shall occur and the number of employees to be laid off. In the event an employee is laid off, that employee will be given priority on the substitute list for which he/she is qualified.

E. An employee with seniority may displace the least senior employee in the same classification or if an employee is not more senior in the same classification the employee may displace the least senior in the next lower classification in the same classification series. The process where an employee with seniority may displace the least senior employee in the next lower classification, in the same series, will continue until there is no more classifications in that series for the employee to displace. Classification series are defined in 5.3(f). An employee may displace another employee in a different classification series if that employee has previously been employed in that classification series as a regular, District employee if all of the following conditions are met:

1. the employee lacks seniority in the classification series of employment at the time of the reduction in force,
2. the employee has seniority in a previous classification series, and
3. the employee is qualified for employment in the previous classification series, both with respect to necessary licensure and physical qualifications to perform job duties in the previous classification,
4. Employees may not bump into a position having a greater number of hours than were assigned the employee in the classification held prior to the exercise of bumping rights.

Seniority is calculated on length of service from the most recent date of hire, adjusted for leaves of absence. Classification seniority means length of continuous service in a classification series, adjusted for leaves of absence.

F. The classification series are as follows:

Auditorium Services:
1. Auditorium Manager
2. Auditorium Technician

Custodial Services:
1. Head Custodian
2. Custodian

Financial Services:
1. Financial Associate
2. Payroll Associate
3. Data Entry Associate

District Food Services:
1. Food Service Manager
2. Cook Manager
3. Food Service Associate

District Maintenance Services:
1. Technical Trades Worker
2. Building Maintenance Worker
3. Landscape Maintenance Worker

Mechanic Services:
1. Head Mechanic
2. Mechanic

Secretarial Services:
1. Administrative Secretary
2. School Financial Secretary
3. District Secretary

The following positions represent classifications for which there are no series:

1. Accounting Budget Coordinator
2. Bus Driver
3. Copy Center Operator
4. Delivery/Warehouse Worker
5. Desktop Technology Technician
6. Educational Assistant
7. Food Service Support Associate
8. Hardware Support Specialist
9. Instructional Technology Integration Leader
10. Library Media Technician
11. Network Specialist
12. Parking Lot Attendant
13. Purchasing Specialist
14. Special Education Attendant
15. Special Education Preschool Attendant
16. Stage Craft Production Technician
17. Technical Systems Information Assistant

18. Technical Systems Operator Support Specialist
19. Transportation Dispatcher
20. Weight room Technician

G. The Superintendent or Superintendent designee shall prepare a reinstatement list for any classification in which a layoff occurs. Employees who are laid off pursuant to this Article shall be recalled in the order of preference group and seniority to positions within the classification in which they were employed when laid off. (For example, the most senior full-time permanent employee laid off in a classification would be recalled first.)

H. An employee who is laid off shall remain on the recall list for eighteen (18) months unless he/she waives recall rights in writing, resigns, fails to accept recall to a position in his/her classification, or fails to report to work within seven (7) calendar days after written notice of recall is sent by certified mail. The employee is responsible for notifying the Board of his/her current address. The Board has complied with this provision when it sends notice of recall to that address. If recalled from layoff, an employee shall retain all previously accumulated seniority, but time spent on layoff shall not count as experience for pay purposes.

I. The Board may deviate from seniority when necessary to meet the requirements of Article 2.8 (Equal Opportunity).

AUTHOR'S NOTE:

LAYOFF AND RECALL. Note that seniority can take a number of different forms. Overall length of service with the enterprise (service seniority) is one, classification seniority, being the length of service in the current, or in some cases, prior job classification is yet another. Like most similar provisions, the layoff process receives a great deal of attention while the callback process is often little more than an afterthought.

Discipline

ARTICLE II - DISCIPLINE

SECTION 1. No bargaining unit member shall be removed, reduced in pay, suspended, reprimanded except for just cause.

SECTION 2. The Employer may take disciplinary action for employee actions which occur on or off duty that violate the established rules and regulations of the Department and/or City.

SECTION 3. The parties recognize the principle of progressive discipline as follows:

1. verbal/written warning;
2. written reprimand;
3. if necessary, a suspension; and
4. if necessary, termination.

Provided, however, the City Manager shall have the right, depending on the circumstances, to either immediately suspend or terminate an employee.

SECTION 4.

(A) The City shall, as soon as possible, before any disciplinary action that results in a suspension or greater, conduct a predisciplinary hearing. The purpose of that hearing shall be to advise the employee of the basis of the discipline. The employee may, if he/she desires, have Union representation at that hearing and also may offer evidence in opposition to the City's charges at that time.

(B) The City shall issue a decision within one (1) week of the hearing. The employee shall have the right to appeal such discipline to the grievance/arbitration procedure.

AUTHOR'S NOTE:

DISCIPLINE AND DISCHARGE. Note that this provision makes "just cause" the sole criteria for disciplining a bargaining unit employee, regardless of the severity of the discipline. Volumes have been written on exactly what "just cause" means in the context of employee discipline, but it is important to understand that the above provision places the burden on the employer to establish that it in fact had "just cause" for imposing the challenged discipline.

Rather than attempting to replicate the scholarly analysis, let me give you my thumbnail version of what "just cause" means to most arbitrators who may ultimately be required to rule on "just cause" discipline. The employer will be required to answer the following questions:

- Was the conduct leading to the discipline harmful to the operation of the enterprise or to the health, safety, or welfare of other employees or a member of the public?

- Was the conduct leading to the discipline prohibited by law or by a work rule that had been established by the enterprise and communicated to the employee?
- If not subject to an express work rule, had the employee been cautioned not to engage in the conduct previously and then engaged in the conduct with knowledge that it was prohibited?
- While there may be circumstances that don't fit the above analysis, if the answers are "yes" to any of the above questions the employer should prevail over a challenge to the discipline, provided that the actual level of discipline imposed is commensurate with the severity of the misconduct. For example, even though being late to work is prohibited, the termination of a twenty-five-year employee who was ten minutes late for work on one occasion is not likely to gain favor with any arbitrator reviewing the discipline.

Sick Leave; Leaves of Absence

ARTICLE 19 - SICK LEAVE

A. CALCULATION OF SICK LEAVE

1. There shall be fifteen (15) days of sick leave per school year for each full-time unit member employed by the Board. Unit members who render part-time, seasonal, intermittent, per diem, or hourly service shall be entitled to sick leave for the time actually worked at the same rate as that granted like full-time unit members. A unit member employed as a substitute with an assignment to one specific teaching position shall, after sixty (60) days of service, be granted sick leave. The basis for determining the number of days of sick leave for full-time unit members shall be one and one-four (1/4) days per month for twelve (12) months. Sick leave shall be cumulative to a maximum of two hundred sixty (260) days. Sick leave above two hundred sixty (260) days can accumulate at the rate of fifteen (15) days per year for the purposes of sick leave only beginning July 1, 2006.

a. Accumulation of sick leave shall be based on the following formula and credited to unit member's sick leave records:

Average Number Hours Worked Per Day	Monthly Accumulation of Sick Leave
6 hrs. 00 min. – 8 hrs. 00 min.	1 1/4 days
4 hrs. 30 min. – 5 hrs. 59 min.	1 day
3 hrs. 00 min. – 4 hrs. 29 min.	3/4 day
1 hr. 30 min. – 2 hrs. 59 min.	1/2 day
45 min. – 1 hr. 29 min.	1/4 day

b.Unit members shall have sick leave deducted according to the following formula:

Amount of Time Absent Per Day	Sick Leave Deduction
5 hrs. 16 min or more	1.00 day
3 hrs. 31 min. to 5 hrs. 15 min.	0.75 day
1 hr. 46 min. to 3 hrs. 30 min.	0.50 day
45 min. to 1 hr. 45 min.	0.25 day

A unit member may arrange coverage for thirty (30) minutes or less with a colleague as long as such coverage is approved by the building principal. No stipend will be paid for coverage(s) in these situations.

2. At the beginning of a full-time unit member contract year, unit members with a cumulative total of less than five (5) days' sick leave will be advanced the number of sick days necessary to bring their beginning total to five (5) days.

3. If a unit member is hired during the school year, he/she shall be credited with sick leave in proportion to the fractional part of his/her term, which remains at the rate of one and one-fourth (1 1/4) days per month.

B. USE OF SICK LEAVE

1.Unit members may use sick leave for absence due to personal illness, disability resulting from pregnancy, injury, exposure to a contagious disease that could be communicated to others, and for illness, injury, or death in the immediate family. For sick leave purposes, immediate family shall be defined as father, mother, sister, brother, husband, wife, son, daughter, grandchildren, grandparents, father-in-law, mother-in-law, sister-in-law, brother-in-law, person or children living in the same household, or another person who has established a similar relationship.

2. Proof of illness or of absence for other reasons must be established with the local Superintendent.
   a.   Each absence of three (3) consecutive days or less must be explained on a form provided by the district office.
   b.   A unit member absent more than three (3) consecutive days, or for any number of days suggesting a pattern of possible sick leave abuse may be required to furnish a satisfactory written, signed statement listing the name and address of the attending physician, and the dates when he/she was consulted, to justify the use of sick leave. This is also to be applied to absence due to illness or injury in the immediate family. The signing and filing of such

absence report by a unit member shall be a certification by him/her that the facts and statements contained in said report are true and correct. The filing of any willfully false statement by a unit member shall be considered by the Board as grounds for suspension or termination of employment under Section 3319.16 of the Ohio Revised Code.

C. OTHER PROVISIONS

1. A unit member planning to request a leave of absence and/or use of sick leave because of disability resulting from pregnancy shall make her request in writing, accompanied with a statement from her doctor indicating the expected delivery date. This request should be made at least forty-five (45) days prior to her expected delivery date. For the purpose of this provision, disability resulting from pregnancy is the period during which the unit member is not physically and/or emotionally capable of performing all the duties, and functions of her position. This beginning date of disability shall be established by written statement of the unit member's doctor. Also, the ending date of the disability shall be established by a written physician's statement.

2. Personnel new to the district having accumulated sick leave in other appropriate Ohio employment, as defined in the Ohio Revised Code 3319.141, may transfer a maximum of one hundred twenty (120) days to the _____. If a unit member is transferring accumulated sick leave from another agency, such employment in that agency must have occurred within the past ten (10) years.

3. Any unit member who uses all his/her accumulated sick leave may substitute unused personal, emergency, or other forms of leave provided for under Section 3319.08 of the Ohio Revised Code. Each regularly employed unit member, who used all accumulated sick leave and personal leave during a school year, shall be entitled to an advancement of five (5) days of sick leave. Such sick leave shall be charged against sick leave subsequently accumulated by the unit member.

4. In accordance with the Comprehensive Omnibus Budget Reconciliation Act of 1985 (COBRA), eligible unit members may continue group term life, hospitalization, surgical, and major medical insurance coverage. The cost of such coverage is to be paid by the unit member.

5. A unit member absent from work in excess of the number of sick leave or other authorized leave days accumulated by the unit member shall receive a salary deduction calculated by dividing the number of days in the unit member's duty year into gross annual salary thus arriving at a per-day deduction.

6. The Superintendent may require that a unit member returning to work after an extended illness, accident, or pregnancy leave, supply the administration with a doctor's statement indicating that he/she is able to return.

7. A member who is pregnant or who is adopting a child may use sick leave pursuant to this section and/or may take unpaid leave for the period of the member's disability. For this purpose,

"period of disability" means the period during which the bargaining unit member is unable to perform the duties of the job as determined by her physician and the provisions of this paragraph. It is presumed that such period extends for a minimum of six (6) weeks beyond birth in the case of birth by normal delivery and eight (8) weeks beyond birth in the case of a birth by cesarean section. The Board may require medical certification, using the prescribed form, if paid leave is requested beyond the applicable presumed period of disability. If the Board questions such medical certification, the Board may have the employee's condition evaluated, at Board expense, by a Board-designated physician. If a disagreement exists between the employee's physician and the Board-designated physician, the employee (with Association assistance) and the Board shall mutually agree upon the selection of a third physician, whose opinion shall be final and the cost of which will be borne by the Board if the physician sides with the employee's physician and by the Association if the physician sides with the Board-designated physician. The Board will not question the medical certification provided by the employee under this paragraph arbitrarily or capriciously.

D. SICK LEAVE TRANSFER

The Board will honor written requests from a bargaining unit member to donate one or more sick leave days from the donor's accumulated sick leave to a member donee under the following conditions:

1. The written request for donation of sick leave shall be forwarded to the Superintendent and the Association President

who shall meet and confer if the request falls into the category of "catastrophic." For purposes of this Section normal pregnancy shall not be considered a "catastrophic" illness. Any disagreement between the Association President and the Superintendent shall be resolved using expedited arbitration in accordance with the voluntary rules of the Federal Mediation Conciliation Services (FMCS). Expenses for the arbitrator's services shall be equally shared by the parties.

    a. Should the Association President and the Superintendent agree that the request falls in the category of "catastrophic," they will forward the request to the Sick Leave Transfer Committee.

    b. Should the Association President and the Superintendent agree that the request does not represent a catastrophic illness or injury, then the request shall be denied. The member will have the right to request expedited arbitration indicated in paragraph A above.

2. Donated sick leave days may only be credited to a donee member who has, or is about to exhaust all of the donee members' accumulated sick leave and personal leave due to a catastrophic illness or injury of the donee member or illness of child and/or spouse of the donee member.

3. Donated sick leave days may only be used for personal catastrophic illness/injury of the donee member, or illness of child and/or spouse of the donee member, and may not be used for the illness of other family member.

4. A sick leave donation form, authorizing the Treasurer to deduct donated sick leave days from the donor member's accumulated sick leave and to credit the donated sick leave day(s) to the donee member will be sent to unit members for completion. Completed forms will be returned to the committee. The committee will provide the Treasurer with a form indicating the number of days to be transferred, from whom, and the name of the recipient.

5. Any request to donate sick leave days to a member must be submitted to the Treasurer not less than fifteen (15) days prior to any payroll that will include payment for the donated sick leave days.

6. Any member who has reached the maximum sick leave accumulation will have his accumulation reduced by the number of sick leave days donated.

7. Requests for sick leave days will be honored only as long as days are available from donors.

8. The following limitations will apply to this section:
   a. No bargaining unit member who begins the school year with less than forty-five (45) days as of July 1 can donate sick days.
   b. Donations from a bargaining unit member must be in units of one (1) day or more provided that the donor does not go under forty-five (45) days of accumulated sick leave.

c. Either the bargaining unit member or the members spouse and/or child must have the catastrophic illness or injury.

d. The bargaining unit member can use donated sick days until disability retirement is effective.

9. No member may use donated sick leave days to defer eligibility for disability retirement under STRS regulations, to claim severance pay, or to transfer to any other public employer.

10. No member may use more than thirty (30) donated sick leave days in total in any year.

ARTICLE 20 - LEAVES OF ABSENCE

A. ASSAULT LEAVE

The Board shall grant paid assault leave to a unit member that is assaulted by a nonemployee of the Board while in performance of his/her duties. In order to receive assault leave, an MD (or licensed medical doctor) shall certify that the unit member suffers disabilities as a direct result of the assault that prevents him/her from performing his/her job. The initial allocation of assault leave will be up to ten (10) days as determined by the unit member's physician. Additional days shall be granted if the need is certified by an MD (or licensed medical doctor).

B. ASSOCIATION LEAVE

1. The Association shall be granted fifteen (15) days of Association Leave per year and twenty-five (25) days per year in contract negotiations years, provided the Association notifies the Superintendent of the name(s) of the unit member(s) taking the leave.

2. If the Association President is not full-time, the Association President shall be granted additional leave of seven (7) days. The President has the authority to transfer any of these seven (7) days to the total in #1 above, during bargaining years. The Association President shall notify the Principal/Superintendent at least twenty-four (24) hours prior to the leave.

3. For the Association Executive Committee members, the leave may be divided into half (1/2) days, as needed.

4. If more days are required for the leave referred to in Sections 1 or 2 above, they may be granted upon approval of the Superintendent, provided the Association reimburses the Board for the cost of the substitute for those additional days.

5. The notice requirements contained in Sections 1 and 2 above may be waived upon the discretion of the Superintendent.

C. CHILD CARE LEAVE

1. A unit member who has given birth or adopted a child shall be entitled, upon request, to an unpaid leave of absence up to

one (1) year. This one year will be available in the following fashion:

    a. delivery/adoption occurs in the 1st semester or during the summer prior to the 1st semester, the unit member may take the balance of the 1st semester and all of the second semester.

    b. delivery/adoption occurs in the 2nd semester, the unit member may take the balance of the second semester and the next full school year on unpaid leave.

    c. The unit member may opt to use unpaid leave until the end of the semester in which the delivery/adoption occurred.

    d. Reference Section J. (contract status and assignment upon return).

2. Applications for child care leave shall be in writing, and they shall contain a statement of the expected delivery date, the requested beginning date of the leave of absence, and the date the unit member desires to return. The application will also contain a physician's statement certifying pregnancy.

3. Applications for childcare leave prior to childbirth shall be made at least forty-five (45) days prior to expected delivery date. In the case of adoption, such application shall be made within ten (10) days of the notice from the adoption agency of the expected placement.

4. Unit members on leave of absence shall notify the Superintendent by letter by April 1 of their plans for the ensuing school year. Such

intent shall not be construed as a formal commitment for the ensuing school year, unless so stated in the letter. This procedure shall be interpreted as a planning vehicle for the school district, rather than an effort to cause a unit member to make a premature decision regarding employment status.

5. Upon request, a father may be granted an unpaid leave of absence for up to one year. The above procedures and regulations shall be observed in such requests.

6. In the case of a childcare leave related to adoptions, the unit member shall:
   a. Notify the Superintendent of his/her intent to adopt when he/she is notified by the social agency that the home study is to commence.
   b. Notify the Superintendent when: (1) the home study has been completed and approved to enable appropriate arrangements for replacement, and (2) request child care leave and indicate the approximate length of such leave.
   c. Upon placement of an adoptive child, the requesting unit member shall be granted five (5) days paid leave as an acclimation period.
   d. In the case of private adoption, the unit member shall notify the Superintendent that application for private adoption has been made and request a childcare leave with an estimate of the beginning and ending date of the leave.

D. MANDATORY COURT APPEARANCES AND JURY DUTY

The Board shall grant a unit member leave for jury duty. The unit member shall receive his/her regular rate of pay and shall be required to notify the Treasurer's Office regarding the amount of monies received from the court less expenses, and pay such amount to the Treasurer, as requested. Members required to appear in court by subpoena as a result of the performance of regular teaching or supplemental duties will be granted leave with pay except when the court appearance is for the purpose of testimony or participation in a matter or proceeding adverse to the Board of Education.

E. MILITARY LEAVE

Military leave shall be granted to unit members according to the Ohio Revised Code.

F. PERSONAL LEAVE

Three (3) personal leave days will be granted each unit member yearly to be used in accordance with the following paragraphs. Part-time, unit members shall have their personal days prorated based upon their full-time equivalent hours worked. Unit members hired after the start of the school year shall be given one (1) personal day for each sixty (60) days contracted.

Personal leave shall be used only for personal business that cannot be conducted at any other time except during the regular school day. Requests for personal leave shall be submitted to the building principal at least forty-eight (48) hours in advance of the day requested.

Personal leave will not be available during the first week and the last three (3) full weeks of school* ending with the last teacher workday, and shall not be used to extend a holiday or vacation period or used three (3) days in succession unless approved by the Superintendent.

If emergency circumstances make it impossible to submit the request in advance, the request must be made by telephone and then confirmed by submission of a completed personal leave form.

Unit members requesting personal leave on the day preceding or the day following a holiday or vacation period, or during the first week or last three (3) weeks of school, must submit the appropriate form along with written reasons for the request. If the request is due to an emergency, personal business, the wedding or the day before the wedding of the unit member or the member's child, or the need to attend a school-related activity of an immediate family member (spouse or child) occurring on a school day which cannot be conducted at any other time except during the regular school day, and is acceptable to the Superintendent or designee, the regular deduction rate will apply. If the reason for the request is not acceptable to the Superintendent or designee, the unit member may take personal leave, but will have personal leave deducted at a rate of one and a half days (1%) per one (1) day of personal leave usage.

Unused personal leave days shall be ***either:***
- Converted to sick leave accumulation or
- Cashed in at a rate of $90 per day (request must be

submitted by April 1 regarding intent to cash in the days vs. converting them to sick leave)

- Payment for unused days shall be included in the first paycheck in August

*The three (3) week period includes the period beginning twenty (20) calendar days prior to the last workday for unit members for a total of twenty-one (21) days.

G. PROFESSIONAL LEAVE

The Board shall, within its financial means, provide opportunities for unit members to develop and improve their skills beyond that which may be attained through their assigned duties. Requests for attendance at conferences outside the State of Ohio and for any conference requiring more than one night of lodging must have prior Board approval. The following procedures and regulations shall be observed.

Such opportunities include the following:
1. Leave of absence for study.
2. Visits to other classrooms.
3. Scheduled meetings involving county school personnel and individuals from other county schools.
4. Various committee responsibilities, which relate to the school district.
5. Workshops within the district.
6. Various other conferences and workshops designed to improve or develop a particular skill.

In planning local staff development programs, such as in-service meetings, every effort shall be made by the groups involved to obtain specialists and materials from state and local agencies, whose services would be at no cost to the Board. The Superintendent/designee shall be responsible for approving expenditures for Staff Development activities within the limits of the appropriation. Requests for attendance at conferences outside the State of Ohio and for any conference requiring more than one night of lodging must have Board approval. The following procedures and regulations shall be observed.

I. CRITERIA FOR ATTENDANCE AT PROFESSIONAL MEETING

The following items should be considered when evaluating requests for attendance at professional meetings:

a. How will attendance enhance the district's continuous improvement goals?

b. How will the _____ schools benefit?

c. How is the meeting or conference appropriate for person making the request?

d. How much time would be lost from work?

e. Are funds available in the appropriation?

f. How many persons are requesting attendance at this meeting or conference?

g. How many meetings has this person attended?

h. Can suitable arrangements be made for the unit member's school responsibilities?

2. VISITATION

Unit members requesting released time of one (1) school day or less to visit other education institutions must complete the Request for Permission to Attend Professional Meetings or Visitation, form #4080.1, and submit it to the appropriate building principal, who may either reject or approve the request in accordance with item #1 above. To qualify for such reimbursement, the request must have the prior approval of the local Superintendent. Normally, not more than one (1) full day of visitation may be granted to a unit member during the school year.

Mileage for such visitations will not be paid by the Board unless both of the following criteria are met:

a. The programs or schools visited are unique or particularly relevant to the _____ Schools and the unit member making such request.

b. The round trip mileage exceeds thirty (30) miles from the unit member's assigned place of work or point of departure.

3. COUNTY OFFICE MEETINGS

Unit members shall be encouraged to participate in appropriate county office meetings, workshops, and activities. Mileage expenses incurred shall be paid by the Board.

4. CONFERENCE/WORKSHOP REIMBURSEMENT PROCEDURES

Conference/workshop attendance rotation and reimbursement procedures shall be established in each building by the Building Advisory Council.

Upon approval, a unit member shall be entitled to reimbursement of the necessary and actual expenses incurred as a result of attending the conferences or workshop, including mileage at IRS established rate. Expenses must be itemized for such costs and submitted with receipts to the Treasurer within thirty (30) days for reimbursement following the unit member's return. Tips and liquor are not reimbursable.

Conference/workshop registrations for unit members will be prepaid up to the amount approved by the respective Building Advisory Council. Should a unit member not attend a conference or workshop, they will reimburse the district for the registration fee portion that was prepaid. This reimbursement will be deducted from the unit member's pay.

For conferences and workshops in which college credit is earned, the district will not reimburse the unit member for expenses associated with both the conference and professional growth college credit. Such reimbursement shall be governed by the following:

a. Head coaches will be entitled, upon approval, to reimbursement for not more than two (2) clinics per calendar year. Total reimbursement for the two (2) meetings, including the registration fees, meals, mileage, and other expenses, shall not exceed three hundred dollars ($300) per coach during the calendar year.

    Assistant coaches may be reimbursed for not more than one (1) clinic for each sport in which the coach is involved, up to one hundred fifty dollars ($150).

b. Unit members will be released from school duties to attend approved conferences or clinics at their own expense, in addition to the above limitations.

c. In the event the evaluation process identifies a unit member quality that could be improved or corrected by attendance at a particular conference or workshop, the school district shall reimburse the unit member up to one hundred percent (100%) of the expenses of said conference.

The Administration has the right to request such attendance at a given conference or workshop that has been identified as being helpful to the unit member.

d. When the Superintendent, in consultation with other appropriate personnel, determines that a unit member needs to develop or improve a particular skill or quality related to the performance of one's duties, then the school district may reimburse the unit member up to one hundred dollars ($100) of the expenses incurred while attending the conference.

5. PROCEDURES FOR UNIT MEMBER INVOLVEMENT AS AN OUT-OF-DISTRICT WORKSHOP PRESENTER OR TOURNAMENT WORKER.

a. Unit members who are to be presenters in another educational institution may use professional leave and the district shall provide the substitute teacher, if any.

b. Unit members who are presenters for any other organization or who are tournament workers may use professional leave provided the District is reimbursed for the cost of the substitute, if any.

c. The unit member may be reimbursed for any expenses incurred such as meals, mileage, and lodging by the organization, but not the Board.

d. If the unit member receives any compensation for presentation(s) or tournament work, that amount shall be divided equally between the unit member and the District. The District shall allocate the monies to the building or department in which the unit member works to be used for that building's programs or for any other mutually agreed upon allocation.

e. No more than two days of leave per unit member per year for presentations and one day per unit member per year for a tournament may be authorized under this section.

H. SABBATICAL LEAVE

1. Upon written application, not later than April 1 of any school year, a unit member who meets the following qualifications shall be granted a sabbatical leave.

2. All applications for sabbatical leaves will be reviewed by a committee consisting of three (3) representatives to be named by the Superintendent and three (3) representatives to be named by the Association President. The committee shall consider, among other qualifications, the following:

a. The proposed program of the applicant as related to professional graduate study, travel, writing, or research.

b. The value of the proposed program to the _____ Schools, its pupils, and the individual applicant.

c. The applicant's total length of service with the _____ Schools.

3. In order to be eligible for a sabbatical leave, a unit member must have been employed in the _____ School District for at least five (5) years.

4. Unit members requesting such leaves must accompany their applications with detailed plans for the proposed use of their sabbatical leaves. Within ninety (90) days after the expiration of his/her leave, the unit member will make a written report to the Superintendent detailing the use, which was made of his/her leave. If the leave was granted for graduate study, the unit member will present to the Superintendent a transcript from the university or college attended.

5. Unit members approved for a sabbatical leave will be notified of their approval by May 15, or as soon thereafter as possible. A unit member on a sabbatical leave shall be given an employment contract for the year of leave and shall be entitled to a salary equal to the difference between their previous salary and the salary of the substitute teacher replacing them while on sabbatical leave.

6. As a condition of being granted a sabbatical leave, a unit member must agree to return to the _____ Schools for a period of one (1) year upon returning from leave. Failure to do so shall require the unit member to refund to the Board all payments received from the Board for sabbatical leave purposes during the leave period. Such refund shall be made within a four (4) month period of time, beginning with the first full month said unit member was to have returned to duty. Such time limit may be extended by agreement of both parties.

7. Unit members on sabbatical leave shall be given full experience credit on the salary schedule and credit for seniority purposes for the period of the leave and shall return to their same or to a similar position as they held at the time the leave commenced.

8. A bargaining unit member on sabbatical leave may maintain health, life, and dental insurance benefits during the period of the leave. Any member desiring continuation of such benefits must notify the Treasurer not less than thirty (30) days prior to the commencement of the leave and pay to the Treasurer an amount equal to fifty percent (50%) of the total monthly cost of the insurance not less than ten (10) days in advance of the time that the Board premium payment is due.

9. Any bargaining unit member who purchases retirement credit for the portion of their salary forfeited during the sabbatical leave will pay to STRS both the employee and employer share of retirement contributions.

10. All such sabbatical leaves shall be granted in conformity to the provisions of Section 3319.131 of the Ohio Revised Code.

I. UNPAID LEAVES

The Board, with the recommendation of the local Superintendent, may grant leave of absence to a unit member with the following stipulations and guidelines being observed:

I. REQUESTS FOR LEAVES OF ABSENCE

All requests for leaves of absence shall be submitted in writing to the local Superintendent through the appropriate Principal. Such requests shall be delivered to the local Superintendent not less than thirty (30) calendar days prior to the requested beginning date of the leave, unless an emergency situation exists as determined by the local Superintendent.

2. TYPES OF LEAVES OF ABSENCE
Leaves of absence shall be granted for the following reasons:
   a. Personal illness
   b. Disability
   c. Professional improvement
   d. Illness in immediate family
   e. Military service
   f. Social Obligations

A leave of absence may be used only for the purposes stated in the written request. Requests for leaves of absence for personal illness, disability, and illness in the immediate family will be granted for the duration of the disability, as determined by the physician. However, a leave of absence may be extended beyond the disability period up to the remainder of the school year upon request of the unit member and if the Superintendent determines that it is in the best interest of the school district to extend the leave.

3. UNPAID DISABILITY LEAVE
Unit members who have exhausted all available sick leave benefits, who are not disabled under STRS disability retirement standards but who qualify for an unpaid leave of absence for medical reasons shall be required to request such leave from the Board of Education, and such leave shall be granted or extended for up to two years.

Unit members who are unable to return to work and who fail

to request such leave, or to return to duty upon the expiration of such leave shall be given written notice by the district treasurer that such action is deemed an abandonment of employment and all further rights to employment in the school district are extinguished.

4. Contract Status

A unit member on a limited contract who has been granted a leave of absence prior to the second semester will have his/her contract run concurrent with the leave. If the contract expires during the leave or if the leave and contract terminate at the same time, the unit member shall be granted an additional one (1) year limited contract. The unit member will return to the appropriate limited contract sequence following a successful evaluation under this one (1) year limited contract.

A unit member on a limited contract, who is on a leave of absence after the start of the second semester whose contract expires during the leave, shall be granted an additional limited contract of the same length as that of the contract currently expiring, provided there has been a successful evaluation completed during the first semester.

5. Assignment Upon Return

The Board cannot guarantee the return of the unit member to the assignment held prior to the leave; however, every effort will be made to return the unit member to a comparable position, acceptable to the unit member.

In cases of a RIF (Reduction in Force) when a leave of absence by a unit member not affected by the RIF would reduce the number of layoffs, that unit member shall, upon request, be awarded his/her former position in the following year as a condition for requesting a leave of absence. Upon return, said position shall not be exempt from the procedures of the RIF policy.

6. COMPENSATION DURING LEAVE OF ABSENCE

All leaves of absence shall be without pay. Upon returning, the unit member shall resume the same level on the salary schedule assigned at the time the leave commenced, unless one hundred twenty (120) days of service had been completed during the year of the leave of absence. The only exception to this is the case of leaves in the Armed Forces of the United States. Such service of not more than five (5) years shall be considered as though teaching services had been performed. Continuation of life insurance will be subject to the carrier's policy provisions.

7. LENGTH OF LEAVE OF ABSENCE

Leaves of absence for any purpose other than military service, may be granted for not more than two (2) years. If the leave commences during the school calendar year, the normal duration of the leave will be until the end of the same school year. In unusual circumstances and upon the recommendation of the local Superintendent, the leave may be extended for not more than two (2) full years.

8. NOTIFICATION OF RETURN

The unit member shall include in his/her request the intended date of return. A leave of absence approved by the Board shall include the starting and ending date of the leave of absence.

All full year leaves will end by the start of the next school year.

Professional improvement leaves will be granted for either one (1) semester or one (1) year only, and a leave of absence for "personal" reasons will not be granted this provision.

J. FAMILY AND MEDICAL LEAVE ACT

Notwithstanding any provision in this Agreement to the contrary, on and after August 5, 1993, each of the parties reserves all rights and responsibilities provided employers and employees under the Family and Medical Leave Act of 1993 (the Act). It is the intent of the parties that all rights regarding leaves provided by the Act shall be solely determined by the provisions of the Act and the regulations adopted thereunder which will supersede and take the place of all related leave provisions contained in this Agreement.

K. RELIGIOUS LEAVE

A unit member may be absent with pay on a religious holiday not included in the school calendar. The holiday must be observed by a bona fide religion or religious body, which has historically observed the religious holiday in such a fashion as to preclude attendance at school. Such absences shall not exceed two (2) days during the school year. A unit member must fill out a Request for Religious Holiday Leave Form at least forty-eight (48) hours in advance of the day requested. The request form shall state the specific religious holiday requested.

AUTHOR'S NOTE:

LEAVES. The leave provisions include both sick leave as well as a listing of both paid and unpaid leaves available to the members of the bargaining unit. Note that the sick leave provision permits unit members to donate sick leave to other bargaining unit members. If presented with such a proposal, keep in mind that donated sick leave is almost always used, thus turning a potential cost into an actual cost as many bargaining unit members, especially teachers, accrue large amounts of sick leave they never use. The second, general, leave section demonstrates how contracted benefits grow from one negotiation to the next. Members could be absent from duty for an entire year or more utilizing negotiated leave provisions.

Union Dues Post-Janus

II.03 PAYROLL DUES/DEDUCTIONS

A. The _____ agrees to deduct from the pay of bargaining unit employees' dues for the Ohio Association of Public School Employees and its Local Chapter 214 when authorized in writing by each employee.

B. The _____ shall transmit monthly said dues along with an accounting of each withholding by name of employee to the OAPSE State Treasurer.

C. Payroll deductions shall be continuous unless membership is withdrawn in a manner consistent with the withdrawal procedures set forth in the OAPSE membership/dues agreement signed by the employee. Notice of withdrawal shall be sent to the OAPSE state treasurer's office: 36805 Oak Creek Drive, Columbus, Ohio 43229, Attn: Membership Department. OAPSE will notify the OCSD Board Treasurer when the dues deduction authorization is properly withdrawn by the employee.

D. Dues shall be deducted in twenty-four (24) equal payments starting with the first paycheck in the new contract. New members enrolled after the first paycheck will pay equal payments in the remaining paychecks.

E. Individual authorization forms shall be signed by the member and submitted by OAPSE on their behalf to the Treasurer.

AUTHOR'S NOTE:

UNION DUES - POST-JANUS. Two different provisions for the deduction of union dues from the salaries of bargaining unit members are offered to highlight the changes wrought by the United States Supreme Court's *Janus* decision. In the first provision, employees who opt not to join or who withdraw from the union are not held responsible for the payment of union dues or agency fees.

Union Dues Pre-Janus

A. ASSOCIATION MEMBERSHIP

1. Association membership is annual with the membership year being September 1 through August 31. Once a member enrolls such membership shall be continuous thereafter for each subsequent membership year unless the individual cancels his/her membership.

B. MEMBERSHIP CANCELLATION

1. Any individual who wishes to cancel his/her membership must notify the Association Membership Chair or the _____ President/designee in writing on the Association Form between August 1 and August 31. A member may cancel his/her membership outside of the aforementioned cancellation period but shall be responsible for all remaining dues and assessments of the current membership year and by such cancellation acknowledges that he/she is forgoing any rights specifically reserved to members of the Association.

C. PAYROLL DUES DEDUCTION

1. The Board agrees to deduct dues from the wages of employees for payment to the Association upon presentation of a written authorization individually executed by any employee. This deduction shall be made free of charge.

2. Monthly payroll deduction of dues shall be forwarded to the _____ treasurer with a printout of each employee for whom deductions have been made.

3. If the dues deduction is not revoked it shall continue. Such revocation must be in writing and submitted by the unit member between August 21 and 31 to the District treasurer with a copy to the Association treasurer. Those employees who have dues deducted in accordance with IV.A.1. and terminate service with the district prior to the end of the dues deduction period (other than due to death) shall have the remaining dues owed deducted from their final paycheck. The amount of the remaining dues owed shall be certified by the Association Treasurer to the Board Treasurer.

4. The Association agrees to indemnify and save the Board harmless against any and all claims that may arise out of or by reason of action taken by the Board in reliance upon any authorization for dues deductions submitted by the Association.

5. Beginning with the first pay in November, deductions shall be made in twelve (12) equal installments. The amount of the dues deduction shall be specified by the Association President and

submitted in writing to the Board's treasurer by September 30 of each year.

D. SERVICE FEE

All bargaining unit members shall remain dues-paying members for the duration of this agreement or pay the service fee as noted below. It shall be the responsibility of the Association to provide a list of fee payers to the Board's treasurer by September 30 each year.

1. Each bargaining unit member who is not a member of the Association shall pay a service fee which shall not exceed the dues paid by members of the Association. Beginning with the first pay period after January 15th, service fee deductions shall be made in ten (10) equal installments. The Association will provide a list of names to the Board's treasurer of those unit members who are not members of the Association and the total service fee to be deducted for each. Newly hired unit members shall have their fees prorated for remaining deductions.

2. If a unit member subject to IV.B. ends employment before all deductions have been made, the remaining fees owed will be deducted from his/her final check. The amount of the remaining fees owed shall be certified by the Association Treasurer to the Board Treasurer.

3. It shall be the responsibility of the Association to prescribe an internal rebate procedure for rebate of monies spent on political or ideological matters opposed by the unit member which are not related to the purposes of enforcing or negotiating the agreement or grievances.

4. The Association agrees to indemnify and save the Board harmless against any judgments for any costs, expenses, or other liability the Board might incur as a result of the implementation and enforcement of this service fee section provided that:

    a. The action brought against the Board must be a direct consequence of the Board's good-faith compliance with this service fee provision provided, however, that there shall be no indemnification of the Board if the Board intentionally or willfully fails to apply (except due to a court order) or misapplies this service fee provision.

    b. The Board notifies the Association in writing and within fifteen (15) days of any claim made or action filed against the Board by the nonmember for which indemnification may be claimed.

    c. The Board agrees to permit the Association or its affiliated organizations to intervene as a party if it so desires, and/or to not oppose the Association or its affiliated organization's application to file briefs *amicus curiae* in the action.

AUTHOR'S NOTE:

UNION DUES – PRE-JANUS. By way of contrast, the pre-*Janus* practice in many states permitted the deduction of Agency Fees (the equivalent of union dues) from members of the bargaining unit who elected not to join the union or otherwise financially support the bargaining effort. The above provision is there simply to demonstrate the contrast.

Negotiations; Contract Language Rollover

ARTICLE V - NEGOTIATIONS PROCEDURE

A. COMMENCEMENT OF NEGOTIATIONS

Either party may give written notice of the reopening of negotiations between 120 days and 60 days prior to the date the Agreement is due to expire.

The initial meeting between the parties will be held within forty (40) workdays of the date of either party's written request.

B. COVERAGE

The Association has bargaining rights for all employees in the bargaining unit regarding wages, hours, terms and other conditions of employment and the continuation, modification, or deletion of an existing provision of the Collective Bargaining Agreement.

C. SUBMISSION OF ISSUES

All issues for negotiations by the Association and the Board shall be submitted in writing at the first meeting. No additional issues shall be submitted by either party following the designated meeting unless agreed to by both parties. Those articles in the existing agreement, which are not proposed to be modified or deleted by either party, shall become a part of the successor agreement.

D. RIGHTS OF INDIVIDUALS

All members of the Association Negotiating Committee shall have the right to express their views during negotiations and shall be free from reprisal or intimidation during and after negotiations.

E. NEGOTIATION TEAMS

The Board and the Association shall be represented at all negotiation meetings by a team of negotiators, not to exceed two (2) members each; however, each side may invite up to three other persons to observe but not otherwise participate at the table. In addition, each party may bring up to two (2) professional consultants not counted in the numbers above to any negotiation meeting provided that notice has been given not less than twenty-four (24) hours in advance. Neither party in any negotiations shall have control over the selection of the negotiation team of the other party.

F. NEGOTIATION MEETINGS

1. Upon written request for a negotiation meeting, either party will have five (5) days to reply to the request. Within ten (10) days after receipt of the reply, both parties will establish a mutually agreeable site, date, and time for the meeting.

2. If the parties agree to a negotiation meeting, which takes place during the normal workday, all employees on the negotiating team scheduled to work during those hours shall be paid their regular hourly rate for the portion of the workday consumed by the meeting.

3. The parties shall meet at places and times agreed upon. Length of meetings as well as times and places of future meetings shall be agreed upon at the close of each session.

4. Each negotiation meeting will be held in closed session.

5. All negotiations shall be completed within sixty (60) calendar days from the first negotiation meeting, unless otherwise mutually agreed by both parties.

G. CAUCUS

Upon the request of either party, the negotiation meeting shall be recessed to permit the requesting party a mutually agreed upon period of time to caucus.

H. EXCHANGE OF INFORMATION

The Superintendent shall furnish the Association, and the Association will furnish to the Superintendent, upon reasonable request, all available public information in the usual form maintained pertinent to the issues under negotiations. Such information shall be submitted to the requesting party not later than seven (7) days from the time of the request.

I. PROGRESS REPORTS

Progress reports, with respect to negotiations, shall be made by the mutual consent of both parties, with the exception of progress reports to the Board and the Association.

J. IMPASSE PROCEDURE

1. In the event an agreement is not reached by the parties, the parties agree to request the use of mediation in an effort to reach an acceptable settlement. The negotiation teams shall request a mediator from the Federal Mediation Conciliation Services (FMCS) whose rules and regulations shall govern the mediation.

2. Either party shall have the ability to declare impasse on those items on which tentative agreement is not reached after a minimum of two (2) mediation sessions have been held.

3. Impasse mediation sessions shall conform to the FMCS rules and regulations.

4. In the event there are costs and expenses for such service the costs shall be shared equally by the Board and the Association.

5. Mediation, as described in Section F and Section J of this Article, constitutes the parties' mutually agreed upon alternative dispute settlement procedure under Section 4117,14 of the Ohio Revised Code and supersedes any and all of the procedures discussed in that statute. Unless mutually extended by the parties, mediation shall terminate at the end of the tenth (10) day following the initial negotiating session after impasse has been declared and which has been held under a mediator's auspices. The Association shall then be entitled to exercise the rights specified in Section 4117.14 (D) of the Revised Code.

K. AGREEMENT FINALIZATION

1. When consensus is reached on those matters being negotiated, the understanding of both parties shall be reduced to writing and submitted to the Association for ratification. Within thirty (30) days from the time the Agreement, ratified by the Association, is presented to the Board, the Board shall take action upon the recommendation submitted.

2. While no final agreement shall be executed without ratification by the Association and the Board, the parties mutually pledge that their representatives will be clothed with all necessary power and authority to make proposals, consider proposals, and make concessions in the course of negotiations. All negotiations shall be conducted exclusively between said teams.

3. When approved by the Board, the Agreement shall be signed by both parties and shall become a part of the official minutes of the Board.

4. All negotiated benefits shall be implemented on the dates stated in the negotiated agreement.

5. Any agreement reached and accepted by the Association and the Board shall supersede any rules, regulations, or practices of the Board which are contrary to or inconsistent with the terms of this Agreement.

6. For the life of this contract the Board and Association each voluntarily and unqualifiedly waives the right, and each agrees that the other shall not be obligated, to negotiate with respect to any subject or matter referred to or covered in this contract and with respect to any subject matter not specifically referred to or covered in this contract, unless otherwise mutually agreed.

L. CONSISTENCY WITH LAW

If any provision of this negotiated agreement shall be found to be unlawful by a court of law having proper jurisdiction, such provision or application shall not be valid, but all other provisions or applications shall continue in full force and effect. Any provision found to be unlawful shall be changed to conform with law through negotiations between the Board and the Association. Such negotiations shall begin not later than thirty (30) days from the parties becoming aware of the court ruling. These negotiations shall take place at the most expedient and mutually agreeable time. Should the parties not reach agreement over the affected provision(s) thirty (30) days after the initial bargaining session, the contractual MAD found in Article V, Section J shall be utilized to resolve the dispute.

AUTHOR'S NOTES:

NEGOTIATIONS. The above provision was likely developed well before the advent of IBB bargaining and is more representative of traditional bargaining. However, most IBB negotiations take place in a fashion contrary to the literal requirements of contracted negotiations procedures, which is fine, so long as both parties agree. I personally disagree with the limitation of negotiations teams to two individuals per side, which seems unreasonably small. However, the inclusion of observers and outside professionals on the team should help blunt the impact of having only two designated bargainers.

CONTRACT LANGUAGE ROLLOVER. As is often the case, this language is not made a separate contract provision. In the above example, it is included in App. 8 at Section C, which provides, in part, "Those articles in the existing agreement which are not proposed to be modified or deleted by either party shall become a part of the successor agreement." As noted in the text, provisions that go into a negotiated agreement seldom come out.

Endnotes

Introduction

1. U.S. Bureau of Labor Statistics news release, January 22, 2021. Union membership represented 34.8 percent of public sector workers, compared with 6.3 percent of workers in the private sector. https://www.bls.gov/news.release/union2.nr0. htm.

2. At the present time, a total of forty-seven states permit some form of collective bargaining for some public-sector employees. "Regulation of Public Sector Collective Bargaining in the States," Center for Economic and Policy Research, 2014. https://cepr.net/documents/state-public-cb-2014-03.pdf. Virginia was added to the list in May 2021. https://news.ballotpedia.org/2021/04/30/union-station-public-sector-collective-bargaining-legal-in-virginia-as-of-may-1/.

Chapter 2

1. See, for example, Ohio Rev. Code Sec. 4117.08 (A).

2. Ohio Rev. Code Sec. 4117.10 (A).

3. See, for example, *Avery v. Midland County,* Tex., 88 S.Ct.

1114, 1117–18; 390 U.S. 474, 479–80 (U.S. Tex. 1968). "The Equal Protection Clause reaches the exercise of state power however manifested, whether exercised directly **1118 or through subdivisions of the State."

4. 585 U.S. ___ (2018), 138 S.Ct. 2448.

CHAPTER 3

1. https://www.fmcs.gov/wp-content/uploads/2019/03/Interest-Based-Bargaining.pdf.

CHAPTER 4

1. A more detailed discussion of the fiscal officer's role is found in Chapter 10.

CHAPTER 5

1. Ohio Rev. Code Sec. 4117.08(A).
2. The term "mature" is used to describe a negotiated agreement that has been renegotiated at least three times.
3. A discussion of grievances and arbitration can be found in Part II, Grievance Procedure.
4. Ohio Rev. Code Sec. 4117.08(A).
5. Impasse is discussed in detail in Chapter 13.
6. Ohio Rev. Code Sec. 4117.08(C).
7. Note, however, that some management decisions, even those clearly within the scope of management rights, can become subject to "effects bargaining" if the decisions have a direct impact on a mandatory subject of bargaining. A discussion of "effects" bargaining is found in Chapter 14.
8. In the section on "effects bargaining" we talk about

circumstances in which an employer may be required to bargain a change in working conditions, even though a contract has been agreed to. The extent to which such obligations can arise will depend on the law governing bargaining obligation in your state.

CHAPTER 6

1. Note that the form of proposals will depend, at least in part, on the bargaining style chosen by the parties.

2. In IBB bargaining the length of the session is usually determined by the mediator.

3. Personal leave is paid time off work allocated as an annual benefit for some teachers.

4. As we noted earlier, it is extremely dangerous for one side of the process to be bargaining in the traditional model while the other side is bargaining in the IBB modes. Don't do it.

5. Usually, each side prepares and retains its own notes, often leading to vastly differing stories about what was intended by contract language when grievances arise over the interpretation of that language. But, if one side has contemporaneous notes and the other does not, the side with notes has a distinct advantage. Grievances can arise years after language has been included in the contract, so it's important to retain bargaining notes going forward.

CHAPTER 7

1. We have addressed mandatory, permissive, and prohibited subjects of bargaining in Chapter 5.

2. In Chapter 9 we talk about "package" bargaining in which

ENDNOTES

both types of issues can be combined into a single proposal that can be agreed to as a package.

3. More about what a caucus is and how it is used will be discussed later in this chapter.

4. I once had a building principal on my bargaining team who insisted on sitting at the end of the table so he wouldn't be viewed as "hostile" to the union's bargaining team members, many of whom worked in his building. Not the best idea, but I understood his perspective.

5. If your team's chief negotiator is not an attorney or otherwise experienced in the drafting of contract language, consider having such an individual available to work with the chief negotiator for the other side in the drafting of contract language to reflect the solutions reached by the IBB bargaining teams.

CHAPTER 8

1. As a general rule, any counterproposal to the union's wage and financial benefit demands will be deferred until much later in the bargaining process for reasons described earlier. However, many other proposals will carry financial implications, and it's important to know the cost of those proposals before submitting counterproposals.

2. An in-depth discussion of the demise of agency fee proposals is included in Part II, Agency Fee.

3. Responses to the union's survey calls to mind a line from the song "Fire Lake" by Bob Seger, "Who wants a raise, who needs a steak?"

4. Though his cause was meritorious, the union contract was not

264

the place to try to prohibit discrimination against pupils, and his proposal was ultimately withdrawn.

CHAPTER 9

1. We discuss the IBB bargaining meeting in Chapter 6.
2. Chapter 10 includes a detailed discussion of dealing with blocking issues.
3. Management's research had established that requests are seldom denied, regardless of the reasons advanced in the leave request.

CHAPTER 11

1. See, https://projectionsinc.com/ unionproofcollective-bargaining-good-faith-impasse/.
2. In rare cases the parties may disagree about whether impasse exists or not. In that case, I usually invite the disagreeing party to make whatever offers it believes that it has yet to make.
3. *ILR Review* – Vol. 17 NO.1 (Oct. 1966).
4. See Chapter 13.
5. In Ohio, for example, fact-finding reports are binding unless rejected by a three-fifths majority vote of the members of either side. Ohio Rev. Code 4117(C) (5).
6. See, for example, Ohio Rev. Code 4117.14(C) (1).
7. See "Last, Best Offer" discussion below.

CHAPTER 12

1. If the tentative agreement includes a provision making the salary increase or benefit retroactive to an earlier time, the adverse effects of a delayed agreement are substantially

reduced. I discourage retroactive provisions for that reason.

2. Note the distinction between "last offer" arbitration discussed in the previous chapter and "last, best offer" here. The "last, best offer" is intended to convey finality and end negotiations. The "last offer" is just that—the "last" offer made.

3. See, Melissa Maynard, "Public Strikes Explained: Why There Aren't More Of Them" Pew Stateline, September 25, 2012. https://www.pewtrusts.org/en/research-and-analysis/blogs/stateline/2012/09/25/public-strikes-explained-why-there-arent-more-of-them.

CHAPTER 14

1. *California Faculty Assn. v. Trustees of the California State University*, PERB case LA-CE-1125-H (Oct. 4, 2012).

CHAPTER 15

1. As a general matter, probationary employment can be terminated at any time, for virtually any reason. Formal discipline for regular employees requires notice and some sort of hearing, a process inconsistent with the notion of probation.

2. See discussion on union dues, below.

3. We earlier cautioned against the use of "interest arbitration," which is arbitration to establish the terms of a collective bargaining agreement. Grievance arbitration is different in that the issue to be decided is whether that agreement has been violated by the conduct complained of, not what the terms of the agreement should be.

4. 29 USC § 2614(a)(4).

5. A word to the wise, "qualification" for a job should be much

more than the subjective judgment of management. A lot of grievances could have been avoided if management had simply taken the time to define the requirements of its jobs and include them in duly approved job descriptions. The posting of any vacancy should either include or reference those requirements as part of the qualification criteria.

6. In Ohio, for example, employees of some school districts are considered civil service employees and may be subject to statutory civil service rules as well as negotiated collective bargaining agreements.

7. Ohio Rev. Code, §§ 3319.08, 3319.081.

8. *Board of Regents v. Roth*, 408 U.S. 564, 33 L. Ed.2d 548, 92 SCt 2701 (1972).

9. 20 USC § 2681.

10. See, for example, 42 USC 2000e-5: Enforcement provisions; Title 42—THE PUBLIC HEALTH AND WELFARE; CHAPTER 21—CIVIL RIGHTS; SUBCHAPTER VI— EQUAL EMPLOYMENT OPPORTUNITIES; http:// uscode.house.gov/view.xhtml?req=granuleid:USC-prelim-ti-tle42-section2000e-5&num=0&edition=prelim.

11. Public Law 103-2, 29 USC § 2601 *et seq.* Under the FMLA. Unpaid leave is available for up to twelve weeks every twelve months.

12. Ohio Rev. Code Sec. 3319.141.

13. See discussion of personal leave in Chapter 6.

14. Deductions were usually provided in order that non-union employees were not required to subsidize the political activities of the local or state-affiliated union.

15. 585 U.S. __ ; 138 S.Ct. 2448 (2018).

16. See, for example, *Pickering v. Board of Ed of Township High School Dist. 205, Will Cty.*, 391 U.S. 563 (1968).

17. This is not to suggest that private employers have carte blanche authority to do whatever they want. They are subject to numerous restrictions both under state and federal law.

18. The *Janus* decision also opens the door to First Amendment challenges to the collective bargaining process by employees claiming that union representation in bargaining infringes their free speech rights. Thus far, the courts appear unwilling to extend the concept to prohibit collective bargaining altogether. *Thompson v. Marietta Education Association*, No. 2:18-cv-00628, 2019 WL 6336825 (S.D. Ohio, Nov. 26, 2019); aff'd, 2020 WL 5015460 (6th Cir. Aug. 25, 2020); cert. denied, 2021 WL 2301972 (S. Ct. June 7, 2021).

About the Author

Nicholas Pittner graduated from Capital University Law School with a Juris Doctor degree, after which he went on to have a successful career spanning over four decades. His professional focus has primarily involved school district collective bargaining and school funding, including litigation on behalf of public school districts. He has received numerous awards, including an honorary Juris Doctor degree from Capital University Law School and being named the Plain Dealer's "Ohioan of the Year" in 2001.

Nicholas currently lives in Ohio with his wife, Susan. They have three children and five grandchildren.

www.ingramcontent.com/pod-product-compliance
Lightning Source LLC
Chambersburg PA
CBHW060332200326
41519CB00011BA/1913